D1521889

The Principal's Edge

by
Jack McCall

EYE ON EDUCATION

EYE ON EDUCATION
P.O. BOX 388
PRINCETON JUNCTION, NJ 08550
(609) 799-9188
(609) 799-3698 fax

Editorial and production services provided by Richard H. Adin Freelance Editorial Services, 96 Rabbit Run Road, Clintondale, NY 12515 (914-883-5884)

Art by permission of the National Policy Board for Educational Administration, 4400 University Drive, Fairfax, VA 22030-4444

ISBN 1-883001-08-0

Library of Congress Cataloging-in-Publication Data

McCall, John R.
        The Principal's Edge / by Jack McCall
                p.   cm.
        Includes bibliographical references.
        ISBN 1-883001-08-0
        1. School management and organization—United States. 2. School principals—United States. 3. Educational Leadership—United States
I. Title.
LB2805.M333   1994
371.2'012—dc20   94-4121
                                                                CIP

Also from Eye On Education:

THE LIBRARY OF INNOVATIONS

Innovations in Parent and Family Involvement
by William Rioux and Nancy Berla

The Directory of Innovations in High Schools
by Gloria Frazier and Robert Sickles

Research on Educational Innovations
by Arthur Ellis and Jeffrey Fouts

THE LEADERSHIP AND
MANAGEMENT SERIES

**The Administrator's Guide to Personal Productivity
with the Time Management Checklist**
by Harold Taylor

Quality and Education: Critical Linkages
by Betty L. McCormick

**Transforming Education Through Total Quality
Management: A Practitioner's Guide**
by Franklin P. Schargel

Eye On Education welcomes your comments and inquiries about current and forthcoming publications. Please contact us at:

Eye On Education
P.O. Box 388
Princeton Junction, New Jersey 08550
(609) 799-9188 phone
(609) 799-3698 fax

ABOUT THE AUTHOR

Jack McCall teaches courses on leadership to public school principals in the Principals' Executive Program at the University of North Carolina at Chapel Hill. A clinical psychologist, he is also the author of *The Provident Principal*, now in its third edition.

At the conclusion of each Principals' Executive Program, the participants select the one principal among them who made the greatest contribution to the learning of the class. That principal receives an honor called the Jack McCall Award.

Table of Contents

FOREWORD

The principalship, properly defined, is a unique collection of knowledge, skills, and attributes. It is not simply a matter of applying technique, such as developing a budget, utilizing management systems, or resolving student conflicts. Unfortunately, we have tended in the past to emphasize technique when preparing principals, rather than developing the fundamental knowledge, skills, and attributes which form the base for any profession, including the principalship.

Jack McCall focuses on the core qualities of the job. He presents these qualities in an informal, engaging manner. Drawing upon classical illustrations and illuminating anecdotes, McCall cuts directly to the heart of what principals must know and do to be effective leaders.

He emphasizes vigorous, hands-on, psychologically sound leadership. In today's organizational environment, there are uncertain expectations for leaders. Readers will appreciate McCall's descriptions and illustrations of leadership skills that are effective in today's site-managed, collegial schools.

The principal's main job is to develop with colleagues purpose and direction, and to move adults and students toward achieving that shared vision. This process demands that the principal develop a host of competencies, clearly defined and explored in this book.

The Principal's Edge affords readers the opportunity to become able school leaders as they enter the job, rather than learning how to be effective afterwards. Furthermore, the book challenges principals to create schools as learning organizations, to give every student a purpose for being in school.

This book provides wise counsel. It is professionally sound and motivational, and brings a wealth of insight and a lifetime of learning to the study of the principalship.

Scott D. Thomson
Executive Secretary
National Policy Board for
Educational Administration

PREFACE

This book is about empowering school principals. I hope to persuade you to read the next 10 chapters and reflect on the questions after each chapter. School principals are key players in the process of changing the way we rear children and adolescents. If the treatment of children in school is to improve, it must start with principals. Principals can't do it alone, but with the leadership of a good principal and the cooperation of many of the stakeholders, any school can improve. This book is aimed at helping principals improve themselves so they will be empowered to improve schools. With improved schools our youth will be better prepared to take their places in the 21st century.

We could write 50 books on school principals and not scratch the surface in explaining this highly complex profession. *The Principal's Edge* takes a more restricted approach. It asks the question, "How do we make a good principal?" Put another way, what suggestions can we offer to help future principals become effective school leaders; and what suggestions can we offer current principals to help them transform their schools into true Learning Organizations?

Before we can answer the training questions, we have to ferret out answers to the question, "What essential knowledge and skills do school principals need to function effectively as leaders?" Until 1993, no one had done this basic research. Now the National Policy Board for Educational Administration, its leader Scott Thomson, editor and consulting editors T. Susan Hill and Beth Mende Conny, offer us information which elucidates the 21 domains of knowledge and skills necessary to programs for new principals and retooling programs for practicing principals. Their research, based on the work of literally hundreds of school administrators, is compiled in a book entitled, *Principals For Our Changing Schools: Knowledge and Skill Base*. I will spend more time discussing that work in our first chapter and will use the directives spelled out in it throughout the *Principal's Edge*.

This book is composed of a series of essays based on the first nine of the 21 domains of knowledge and skills which the National Policy Board for Educational Administration recommends as essential for practicing principals. I won't try to repeat the massive body of knowledge which the National Policy Board study has uncovered. Rather, I will use it as a guide and suggest ways each particular domain of knowledge or skill can be attained, maintained, and enhanced by principals.

I call each of the chapters "essays" (from the French *essayer*, "to try") because that is precisely what they will be—attempts to communicate to principals insights from my personal experience (70 consecutive years in school as learner/teacher/learner) on each of the nine domains. The last 10 years of my life have been dedicated to training principals in the Principals' Executive Program for North Carolina directed by Robert Phay at the University of North Carolina at Chapel Hill. It has been a privilege to be a colleague of Robert Phay, and I have marveled at the skill with which he has founded, directed, nurtured, and inspired this 180-hour residential program. To date, 40 graduating classes with over 1,500 principals have participated. I have been fortunate enough to be able to teach every one of the classes in the program. This means that more than 67% of the public school principals in North Carolina have conversed with me during more than 6 hours of seminars and discussions in their PEP experience. Working with them has been a marvelous revelation. Many of the insights I gathered from these inspiring principals will be used throughout *The Principal's Edge*.

These essays are informal with no scholarly footnotes. They are reflective, rather than prescriptive. I call the book *The Principal's Edge* because appreciation of the nine domains of knowledge and skill developed in this book will give the principal an advantage. The principal who masters these domains of knowledge and skill will have a real edge in running an effective school.

My thanks go to Robert Phay, director of the Principal's Executive Program at the University of North Carolina at Chapel Hill, for his inspiring leadership, and to all his staff and principals who are such a vital part of PEP; and to my publisher, Robert Sickles, and editors Maggie Rosen and Richard Adin, three professionals whose interventions have improved the book considerably. Finally, I would like to dedicate the book to my wife, Mary Hanley, my partner in life-long learning and to all the principals I have taught and hope to teach.

Once upon a time, two loggers had a contest to determine who could cut the most logs in a 4 hour period. Henri worked continuously for 4 hours without a break and cut 124 logs to specification. His opponent, Jacques, chopped just as hard but for only 50 minutes of each hour. Jacques took four 10-minute breaks but yet cut 144 logs to specification. Henri lost the contest and was furious. Henri complained that he was cheated since Jacques could not have cut that many logs because there were periods in which he was not chopping. Then Jacques explained that during his breaks, he didn't rest. He sharpened his axe. That is what gave him the edge. He didn't work harder—he worked smarter. If you read the next 10 chapters, you will work smarter and get more done in changing your school into a Learning Organization. You will certainly gain the principal's edge.

Jack McCall
January 23, 1994

1

THE MAKING OF A PRINCIPAL

Einstein's Three Rules of Work:
(1) Out of clutter find simplicity; (2) From discord make harmony;
(3) In the middle of difficulty lies opportunity.

A public school principal must be a jack or jacqueline of all trades and a master of about 21. Ask your typical middle school principal with a school population of 1,000 students and 100 full-time adults on the staff, what he or she does during an ordinary school day. Most will respond by asking, "How much time do you have to listen?" The chore list includes plumbing, electricity, heating and cooling, a leaky roof, two broken windows, a duplicating machine that just won't work 2 days in a row, sick and hungry kids, irate parents and complaining neighbors, the Board of Health present to inspect the food area, the Environmental Protection Agency representative who wants to check the pollution-lead and asbestos levels, two complaining teachers, two teachers chronically absent, a custodian who disciplines students, not to mention the parking area problems and the buses. This only scratches the surface. High school is worse.

Notice I did not include handling student disciplinary problems, designing and redesigning the curriculum, improving instruction, building a team, motivating teachers and other staff, doing performance appraisals, contributing a vision, modeling patience and kindness. We have not yet reached the forms for central office, report cards, notices of extracurricular activities, sports, dance, theatre, arts, science fair, health fair, dental fair, fund raisers. Nor the calls to parents, return calls from parents, central office supervisor to come visit, staff development program implementation. Don't forget the celebrations for Thanksgiving, Christmas, Valentine's Day, Martin Luther King Day, Grandparents Day, Presidents Day, make up for snow days, the police want to check the metal detector at the front of the school, text books are missing, some vandals have damaged three computers, there most definitely is smoke coming from both basement bathrooms right now. So when you ask a principal," What did you accomplish today?," be prepared for a rather confused look.

Granted all these mishaps don't occur every day. There are enough of them every day to give the best intentioned principal reason enough for not spending time reflecting on the ways to renew the school. Schools will change only as principals learn to dig themselves out of the overload of operations, and find time to really think, dream, brainstorm with peers, interact with students and teachers, read, listen, and visit other schools, so they can envision change in their own school. The school has to be reinvented to meet the demands of our times and schools can't change unless principals change. Principals can't change unless they can accomplish their work in a smarter, less time consuming way. Only then can they become social architects, facilitators of change.

ONLY INFANTS REALLY LIKE CHANGE—WHEN THEY ARE COLD AND WET

All this would go away, and life would be simpler for principals, if they just gave up on change and settled in their comfortable rut. It is a seductive idea. Blast change! Let's just stay the way we are and wait until the world turns a few more times, and we find ourselves leading again.

Schools are not the sole cause of any of our social problems, but schools like all other agencies that touch families and workplaces must change if our social order is to change. Schools must change simply because the present educational system isn't working. Most principals in their forties and fifties were not trained to be change agents. It isn't fair, but it is necessary that these same principals now lead the very changes they were trained to fight against. No one has justly criticized Jefferson for being too liberal or change-oriented, but this great father of our country makes clear his position on change.

> "I am not an advocate for frequent changes in laws and constitutions. But laws and institutions must go hand and hand with the progress of the human mind. As that becomes more developed, more enlightened, as new discoveries are made, new truths discovered and manners and opinions change, with the change of circumstances, institutions must advance also to keep pace with the times. We might as well require a man to wear still the coat that fitted him when a boy as civilized society to remain ever under the regimen of their barbarous ancestors."

Thomas Jefferson, who fought so hard to get the farmers to let their children be free from work in the fields for 3 hours a day to get some schooling, would certainly want us to change schools today. He would point out that less than 2% of the United States' population is engaged in supplying farm products to the other 98%. He would expect us to stop following an agricultural calendar in postindustrial 1994. Jefferson didn't love change for change's sake, but he did see that institutions had to advance and keep pace with the times. Since he had such reverence for schooling, he would certainly urge principals to face up to their Leadership Challenge. The High School class of 2006 is already in Kindergarten.

LEADERSHIP CHALLENGE

Leadership requires changing the "business as usual" environment. Any principal with more than 2 years experience knows how hard it is to get the stakeholders in a school to be willing to change their way of doing business. Teachers like to teach the way they are teaching, students like to study the way they study, parents want the schools to stay exactly as they were when they went to school. School boards dread innovations.

Assuming that schools must change, it becomes apparent that the school can only change if the principal is a real leader. The principal is the "princeps." In Latin that means the chief. A principal by definition is a leader. In a time of social change, every good principal becomes a social architect designing and redesigning a "learning organization." In the next chapter we try to see why the National Policy Board decided to list Leadership as the first of the 21 domains necessary for every principal. Like sunlight directed through a prism, leadership fans out into all the other domains. All other domains contribute to leadership.

MAKING A PRINCIPAL INVOLVES MUCH LEARNING

In an earlier book I wrote, entitled *The Provident Principal*, I also chose Leadership as the first area I would develop. Then it seemed to me that the Values of the principal would be next in importance. A chapter on what change was all about and how it could be accomplished followed. Later chapters dealt with the personal and emotional development of the principal and I offered suggestions on ways the principal could cope with stress. The last chapters were devoted to the changing of an *ordinary* school into a *satisfactory* school in which civility would be the keystone. Finally, I tried to explain how a new way of looking at teaching could help teachers and other stakeholders introduce academic changes into the school. My goal was to explain how *satisfactory* (civil) schools could become *effective* (academic-learning) schools under the leadership of good principals. Since 1984, when *The Provident Principal* was published, every principal in North Carolina who has made the Principals' Executive Program has used this book for discussions and seminars. I have revised it twice and it is now in its fourth printing. Most of the principals seem to like it because I try to speak directly to them about the issues important for their professional growth and development.

Since principals have limited time for study, I delayed writing this follow-up book, hoping that one day reputable people in the field of Educational Administration would do a serious "needs analysis" to find out what exactly it is that principals should know and be able to do in order to be effective leaders of effective schools.

You can imagine my delight when I came into possession of *Principals For Our Changing Schools*. This is the book that I had been waiting for. Let me tell you, in summary fashion, what the authors did, how they did it, and why it is so important to all of us.

The National Policy Board for Educational Administration is the group that saw the problem: "How do we *make* or perhaps better *prepare* an effective principal, one suited to be a real leader in our changing schools?" Scott D.Thomson, the editor, with the help of T. Susan Hill and Beth Mende Conny, consulting editors, designed a procedure which would bring together motivated and informed people to find the answer to this burning question: how can we improve our schools by improving the effectiveness of principals?

It was assumed that the knowledge and skill base of a profession should provide a platform for practice. It also should address core professional responsibilities so that the aspiring principal qualifying for practice could fulfill the essential tasks of the profession in various contexts. Unfortunately, up until this time the educational administration profession had found it impossible to develop the kind of knowledge base that would adequately meet these specifications. In simple language, the experts in educational administration had no practical way of determining what should go into the preparation of a person who was seeking to qualify as a principal. They didn't know much more than I did about giving principals the best possible training. My hit and miss way of choosing material for my book, *The Provident Principal*, was state of the art in 1984, simply because at that time no serious investigation had been made to find out what knowledge and skill base was best for the principals.

In the professions of medicine, law, and architecture, the practitioner has easy access to literature in his or her field. In the professional journals they can find articles of applied research which give them guidance in solving their current professional problems. These articles, written by fellow practitioners, offer current knowledge about many problems being faced in the field. The literature helps these professionals to grow and adapt.

Principals, and those aiming to be principals, are becoming as fortunate as doctors and lawyers. They are starting to find answers to their practical problems in the educational literature. Professors of Educational Administration have begun to write excellent articles of the applied research type. They include current knowledge about how to solve the problems faced by practicing principals. The professors in university Departments of Education are working closely with the practicing principals and, as a result, are able to offer practical guidance, just as the Law professors and professors in Medical School do. Many of the contributors to *Principals For Our Changing Schools* are professors of Education and the material they offer under each of the 21 domains is just the type of practical guidance principals have been hoping for. The publication of *Principals For Our Changing Schools* is the watershed. We now embark on educational renewal with all the players in place. Principals need the applied research being contributed by the universities.

At PEP the principals ask for more classes in School Law. In these classes, the presenter, a lawyer, takes a professional school approach and treats the principals as colleagues grappling with professional problems. The lawyer teaching the course has had to learn a lot about schools and school problems. He or she has real respect for the decisions that the principals must make. The lawyers use cases and examples, encourage questions, initiate discussions on conflicts of interest. The principals act like professionals. They bring out some of their fears about negligence, reporting on sexual harassment, child abuse, etc. The class has a different tone. It seems more real.

Principals have major responsibilities for meeting the educational and developmental needs of their students. They have to continuously initiate action and respond to complex problems. Clearly, technical skill alone is insufficient. So, too, is a complete reliance on content knowledge. The heart of professional practice lies between these two poles—technical skill and knowledge. These were the conclusions reached by Scott Thompson and his team as they began their quest for what a principal should know and do.

They concluded, "New principal preparation programs must address the troublesome 'clinical gap' that exists between classroom and practice, and between subject content and specific technique. To close this gap, a new starting point is required. Accordingly, the search for a knowledge and skill base should begin with the work of principals in contemporary schools. That work must first be defined and organized into identifiable, rational building blocks that are skill-rich and knowledge-rich. Next, the connections between knowledge and skills should be recognized in the many problems principals respond to and in the many tasks they initiate." (1)

In the preface of *Principals For Our Changing Schools*, Scott Thomson writes: "The principalship, like any professional knowledge base, does not represent simply a body of subject content. It consists of knowledge and skills organized in a useful way, preferably into work-relevant patterns that make expert knowledge functional. The professional preparation of principals, therefore, should instruct candidates broadly yet provide them—through classroom format, clinical practice, and field experience—with the practical knowledge and skills they need to address the daily challenges they will face. This approach does not preclude inquiry; rather it channels it in beneficial directions." (2)

These pioneers acknowledge that it is impossible in our changing schools to prepare inexperienced principals for every exigency they will face. So they admit that priority in preparation programs should be given to generalizable knowledge and skills that address new situations and traditional patterns. For example, key interpersonal skills, like oral and written expression or motivating others, and core functional skills, like problem analysis and data-based decision-making, work to a principal's advantage or edge in solving unanticipated problems or, better still, in preventing problems and reversing negative developments.

IT STARTED WITH THE CONVICTION OF 10 SPONSORS

We are told that the genesis of *Principals for Our Changing Schools: The Knowledge and Skill Base,* was a conviction by the 10 sponsors of the project. Remember I said I was waiting for a study by reputable Educational Administration leaders which would give me the confidence that the experts had seriously studied the problem and arrived at solid conclusions. It was something I couldn't do. It was not something one expert or even a team of experts could do. But suppose the 10 sponsors of the National Policy Board for Educational Administration could agree on this proposition: most preparation programs for school leaders reflect a shopworn theoretical base and fail to recognize changing job requirements. Then suppose these 10 prestigious groups pooled their resources and put their considerable weight behind the solution to the problem, then we could recast preparation programs for principals and make them more suitable to the contemporary model. That is exactly what happened.

WHO WERE THE 10 SPONSORS OF THIS MAJOR PROJECT?

Sponsors for the project included The American Association of Colleges for Teacher Education, The Association of School Business Officials, The Council of Chief State School Officers, The National Association of Secondary School Principals, The National School Boards Association, The American Association of School Administrators, The Association for Supervision and Curriculum Development, The National Association of Elementary School Principals, The National Council of Professors of Educational Administration, and the University Council for Educational Administration. What a list! That is the big 10. If you can get all these powerful groups to admit that the present preparation of principals reflects a shopworn theoretical base and fails to recognize changing job requirements, you have made a giant step in the direction of improving the preparation of principals. All that would remain would be a study which pointed out new and better ways to prepare principals. The National Policy Board has done just that with the 21 domains outlined in *Principals for Our Changing Schools.*

How to Go about this Monstrous Task?

The first step in recasting preparation programs for principals into a more contemporary model consists of finding out what the tasks of today's principals are. This is where I become interested. I have been listening to 1,500 principals over the last 10 years express their frustrations. They have tremendous responsibilities, but they don't have the resources to successfully confront them. The National Policy Board segmented the principalship like letters in an alphabet. Each letter, or current task, was analyzed and then replaced into a revised alphabet that also incorporated emerging responsibilities caused by social conditions. The revised alphabet, which included the knowledge and skills essential to the tasks, allowed the building of new paragraphs to describe the contemporary principalship.

The strategy used to form a new knowledge and skills base involved viewing the principalship from two perspectives: inductive and deductive. That meant using inductive task analysis and deductive theoretical analysis and integrating the results. *The outcome constitutes the core of what a principal must know and be able to do professionally.*

What Does a Principal Have to Know and Do?

In the *Principals for Our Changing Schools*, we learn that what a principal has to know and do is encompassed in 21 "domains." Eleven of these "domains" are process or skill oriented; 10 are more content focused; most, however, synthesize knowledge and skill. Some of the "domains" are broad, others are narrow. Some are more central to student-adult relationships; others involve adults only.

I list the 21 domains here, and will develop the first nine in this book.

I. Functional Domains

These domains address the organizational processes and techniques by which the mission of the school is achieved. They

provide for the educational program to be realized and allow
the institution to function.

1. Leadership
2. Information Collection
3. Problem Analysis
4. Judgment
5. Organizational Oversight
6. Implementation
7. Delegation

II. PROGRAMMATIC DOMAINS

These domains focus on the scope and framework of the
educational program. They reflect the core technology of the
schools, instruction, and the related supporting services,
developmental activities, and resource base.

8. Instruction and Learning Environment
9. Curriculum Design
10. Student Guidance and Development
11. Staff Development
12. Measurement and Evaluation
13. Resource Allocation

III. INTERPERSONAL DOMAINS

These domains recognize the significance of interpersonal
connections in schools. They acknowledge the critical value of
human relationships to the satisfaction of personal and
professional goals, and to the achievement of organizational
purpose.

14. Motivating Others
15. Interpersonal Sensitivity
16. Oral and Nonverbal Expression
17. Written Expression

IV. CONTEXTUAL DOMAINS

These domains reflect the world of ideas and forces within which the school operates. They explore the intellectual, ethical, cultural, economic, political, and governmental influences upon schools, including traditional and emerging perspectives.

18. Philosophical and Cultural Values
19. Legal and Regulatory Applications
20. Policy and Political Influences
21. Public Relations

SUMMATION

These are the 21 domains which encompass what a principal should know and do in our changing schools. To appreciate them, you have to read the book, *Principals for Our Changing Schools*. The authors modestly state that their intent has been to define the center lane in a broad road, to identify the essential knowledge and skills for successful practice, and to encourage others to build on this work according to individual and institutional preferences and state licensing. They made sure that all levels of the educational hierarchy would have input into these discussions.

My modest contribution will be to take the first nine of these domains and try to suggest some practical ways for principals to become more knowledgeable and skilled. In a subsequent book I hope to develop the "second nine." I don't touch the last three domains because they cover highly specialized areas on which I could have very little to say.

As I take up each of the domains I will take advantage of the research done by the National Policy Board. I will refer you to the places from which with permission, I have quoted from the book, *Principals for Our Changing Schools*. I have quoted liberally in this chapter from the preface of that work. My hope is that when you have read, studied, and used as a reference *Principals for Our Changing Schools*, you will then turn to this book, *The Principals Edge* for some insights on how to understand and incorporate the first nine domains of knowledge and skills. Given the banquet of goodies provided by the National Policy Board, we have to learn how an individual principal, a group of principals, or a Principals' Academy can get the most from this study.

I will be speaking to you more on a personal level and sharing with you my insights garnered in 70 consecutive years of pleasurable work in schools. It will be from my background in Clinical Psychology and the Liberal Arts, and leaning heavily on my 10 years experience teaching and learning from school principals, that I will try to share some ways of changing schools by changing ourselves.

As we move to Chapter 2, "The Principal's Leadership Challenge," you can do your own self-study or analysis. I have taken the liberty of including after each chapter a few questions that might help you reflect on what has been discussed in that chapter.

There is one theme or thread woven through all 21 domains. The theme is inquiry and advocacy. The principal who is learning how to inquire and to advocate will need to reflect, to question self as well as others in a Socratic manner, and to express his or her ideas clearly and succinctly, both orally and on paper. At PEP we have found that the principals profit greatly from courses aimed at improving their writing and speaking skills.

Every school must have a principal who is truly the "principal teacher" in that school. A principal is the school leader, not merely its administrative or clerical head. Mortimer Adler reminds us that the word "principal" is an adjective and an adjective needs a noun. The noun that goes with principal is teacher. In English schools, the equivalent of our principal is called headmaster or headmistress. With more emphasis being placed on site management, the role of the principal becomes even more crucial. Without the principal there is no school at all. Only a good principal can create a learning community or a Learning Organization. In the next chapter, I will suggest ways that principals can enhance their leadership skills.

Disraeli expressed the leadership dilemma when he said, "I must follow the people. Am I not their leader?" He might have added, "I must lead the people. Am I not their servant?" The same remark is attributed to Ghandi and other famous leaders. What all great leaders have in common is their understanding and acceptance of their colleagues, their willingness to serve them as they move together in pursuit of a Shared Vision.

QUESTIONS FOR REFLECTION

1. Why are so many people more willing to talk about changing themselves and their institutions than they are ready, willing, and able to initiate these changes and follow through on them?

2. Does the metaphor "social architect" capture for you the role of a principal in the midst of trying to change a school? If so, why so? If not, why not?

3. Articles published in journals meant for Educational Administrators appear to many principals to be less helpful to them than the articles written in Medical and Law journals appear helpful to physicians and lawyers. How would you account for that discrepancy, if indeed it exists? Or put in another way, how do the lawyers who teach in Law Schools, and the doctors who teach in Medical Schools handle things differently than the educators who teach in Education Schools?

4. How might it affect our attitudes toward school principals if we referred to them as practitioners, the way we do with lawyers and physicians, instead of thinking of them as school managers? Lawyers practice the Law. Physicians practice Medicine. What do principals practice? Aren't principals really practitioners of teaching and learning? How much time do they spend on that practice?

5. The heart of the principal's professional practice lies between technical skill and knowledge. How are these alike and how are they different? In your opinion, what has characterized your training as a principal up until now? Has the emphasis been more on skills or knowledge? How would you explain the imbalance if it exists?

6. Why have most programs designed to train principals as school leaders shied away from hands-on experience and praxis in favor of courses of an academic and theoretical nature? The word "practice" in education is reserved for undergraduate education majors who are contemplating

school teaching as a profession. Once hired as a teacher, we give practice sessions to the students but we don't think of ourselves as practitioners. Why?

7. As you read over the 21 domains of knowledge and skills I quoted from *Principals For Our Changing Schools,* which ones captured your attention and held it longest? Select from the list the five skills and knowledges you feel are your strongest. Now choose the five in which you need the most help.

2

THE PRINCIPAL'S LEADERSHIP CHALLENGE

Five of Thomas Jefferson's commandments:

1. Never trouble another for what you can do yourself.

2. Pride costs more than hunger, thirst, and cold.

3. Nothing is troublesome that we do willingly.

4. Take things away by the smooth handle.

5. When angry count to 10 before you speak; if very angry, count to 100.

In my past reading, I once came across a book that has over one hundred definitions of leadership. I can't remember even one of them and, moreover, I can't find the book. After sifting through many books on leadership and 55 years of trying to lead, I have arrived at the kind of definition of leadership that works for me.

Leadership is the art of getting others to want to do something that you yourself are so convinced ought to be done, that you have thrown your whole self 100% into the task of trying to accomplish it with their help.

15

"WHAT IS LEADERSHIP?," ASKED THE PRINCIPAL
(A QUESTION NEVER ASKED)

No principal I have ever talked with asked me the question, "What is leadership?" I think all principals know that their job is one of leadership. Some feel more comfortable than others in exercising leadership skills. No two of them lead in exactly the same way. Some are charismatic but the vast majority are more like corn flakes—solid but not flashy. Almost all the principals I know wish they knew more about leadership, but they are even more desirous about improving their leadership skills. If I asked a principal which of the remaining 20 domains of knowledge and skills would help him or her in leading, he or she would answer that all of the remaining domains enhance leadership.

For years we argued in Psychology about whether leaders were born or made. It was much like the inane debate over whether teachers are born or made. I'll bet you a dollar to a donut that more principals are becoming real leaders today in the United States than was the case 25 years ago. Why? Because the times call for leadership. When a society is in turbulent movement and all the agencies and institutions in it are being challenged, the people who are in positions of authority either rise to the occasion and become real leaders or fail in their mission. In such cases, informal leaders take over.

Now that we are encouraging site management in the schools, principals can no longer hide. With site management, crises arise and are settled at the building level. The more site management, the more the principal must lead. Crises can bring out the best in a principal, or reveal his or her "achilles heel".

I regularly see examples of ordinary principals who are accomplishing extraordinary results because they were prodded by crises to develop their leadership potential. We have no idea what we can accomplish until we are forced by the situation to reach beyond our grasp. I see some principals starting Year-Round Schools, introducing flexible scheduling, delegating, doing honest self-studies, pushing team teaching and cooperative learning, introducing outcome-based education, and a multitude of innovations.

Twenty-five years ago there were principals with the same kind of potential leadership, but the situation in the United States was different. Granted the good regional changes engendered by desegregation, it was not the time for radical change at the site level in classroom teaching and learning. Different principals became leaders 25 years ago when the schools were called to desegregate. There were some heroes among them who really faced up to great opposition while implementing the change in law. However, they were not called on to change their school into a Learning Organization. They were courageous implementers of mandated changes.

Different principals will change schools today. They will change the teaching and learning so drastically that never again will we see a report from the U.S. Department of Education which states that half of the adults in this country can't read or handle arithmetic. New principal leaders will share four things in common: They will be in authority when there is a loud call for change across the country. They will have the courage to see when things are broken and be willing to fix them. They will be able to share a vision which will make the necessary changes possible. And, finally, they will be able to get others to want to do what they, the principals, see as the right thing to do. Principals today are becoming leaders by throwing themselves 100% behind the movement for change, and modeling for all stakeholders what selfless leaders are all about.

LEADERSHIP: ON THE JOB LEARNING IS NECESSARY BUT NOT SUFFICIENT

Most people agree that "Leadership" is the most studied and least understood of the key topics in the Social Sciences. We know a lot more about managing than we do about leading. We have many good theories of leadership but it is difficult to apply the theories to the real life situations. Most schools are overmanaged and underled. As we noted earlier, principals are anchored to operations. Just keeping the school afloat takes most of their time and all of their energy. They are forced to handle the little crises of the daily routine, yet they never question whether the routine should be done at all. They often do well things that need not be done at all.

Once I asked a successful superintendent of schools what he
thought of a certain principal, who he was sending to the PEP
program at Chapel Hill. His answer stunned me. He said,
"Jerry is one of my most conscientious principals. He works
hard and long; gets along well with staff, students, and parents;
gets his paperwork done correctly and promptly; and yet he
disappoints me." "How's that?" I asked in some consternation.
"Well," said the superintendent, "Jerry disappoints me because
he could do so much more. He manages well but shows no
signs of initiative, creativity, or real leadership. He does
meticulously and flawlessly the routine things that are a part of
management, but he has no vision. He inspires no one. He
empowers no one. He builds no team. He motivates no one by
modeling, leading, influencing, and guiding in the direction of
a vision for change. Any change that comes to Jerry's school
must come from outside. Jerry is afraid of change. He fears
taking risks. That is why he disappoints me daily, and yet he
can't understand why I don't praise him more for his
perfectionistic handling of routine matters. He was devastated
when I didn't nominate him for 'Principal of the Year.' Jerry
can't learn to be a leader merely with on-the-job training. He
needs a lot more. I am sending him to the Principals' Executive
Program with the hope that you guys can light a fire under
him, and help him to become the leader he is capable of
becoming."

I have heard this story about principals who manage well
but won't lead hundreds of times. Managers are people who do
things right, but leaders are people who do the right things—
activities of vision and judgment.

Three years after Jerry completed his 180 hours of
residential training with 39 other principals in PEP, he had
become a changed man. He really did take chances. He had
developed a network of classmates from PEP whom he called
frequently for support and encouragement. He would bring
two or three of his teachers on visits to the innovative schools
run by some of his PEP colleagues.

This year Jerry and a group of his teachers are seriously
talking about starting a Year-Round School within a school. He
has been seeking information from the community, and
meeting with groups to explain what this quantum leap in

schedule change might do to help bright students be enriched, and failing students get remedial help without waiting 7 months for summer school. Jerry has become a real leader. The old superintendent has gone to a bigger system. The new superintendent assumes that Jerry was always a leader. He couldn't believe what a "stick in the mud" Jerry used to be.

Is this an isolated incident? No way. Of the more than 1,500 principals and 280 assistant principals I have dealt with in the PEP and APEP (Assistant Principals' Executive Program) sessions, I could fill this book with stories like Jerry's. On the job is a great way to become a leader, because leadership has to be done in the real world, but principals need time off the job in order to learn the knowledge and skills on which leadership is based. A Principals' Academy or a program like UNC's can really help principals change their world view. They really surprise everyone including themselves. I foresee the day when principals will be given sabbaticals—a semester off every 7 or 8 years (like college professors) so they can pursue more learning and growth in their professional lives.

THE NATIONAL POLICY BOARD PUTS LEADERSHIP FIRST

The Board puts Leadership in the number one place among the 21 domains of knowledge and skills needed to help principals. Suppose we look at the definition of Leadership supplied by *Principals for Our Changing Schools*:

> *Leadership: Providing purpose and direction for individuals and groups; shaping school culture and values; facilitating the development of a shared strategic vision for the school; formulating goals and planning change efforts with staff and setting priorities for one's school in the context of community and district priorities and student and staff needs.* (3)

The principal's main job is to function as provider of school purpose and direction. The superintendent was disappointed in Jerry precisely because Jerry failed in providing purpose and direction. He didn't have a vision so he couldn't share a vision or get the attention of the stakeholders in the school. Teachers, students, and parents will follow a leader whose values are embodied in a plausible vision. The principal has to be able to explain the vision and convince people that the vision has a good chance of being realized. Before he saw the light, Jerry's values were in details. Jerry couldn't see the big picture. He didn't motivate or inspire teachers and students simply because people don't get fired up over details. Not many of us get gung ho over dotting i's and crossing t's. Now Jerry knows that a vibrant vision replete with noble values will gain the attention of followers, and enlist them to the point where they will freely commit themselves to make cooperative sacrifices for a much greater "good." Jerry has become a vital leader.

LEADERSHIP STARTS WITH CHALLENGING THE STATUS QUO

Some writers like to start talking about leadership by introducing concepts like vision and values. I like to hold back on these necessary ingredients until after we have established something more fundamental. *The first step in leadership is to perceive accurately the present situation.* Jerry, the meticulous manager, obviously did not perceive his school as it really was. If he had, he would have perceived a gap between where his school was and where it ought to have been. Then he would have seen that doing routine work efficiently would not make his school more effective. Only when his perception cleared, did he come up with the new vision.

Human perception suffers from a mismatch between our slow to evolve brain and our rapidly advancing ability to use technology in changing our environment and habitat. How else to explain the way we humans pollute our air, water, and land? Recently, the Hudson River above West Point has become swimmable. For years it was polluted by chemicals poured into it by factories whose CEOs either didn't know what effect their poisons would have on fish and humans or didn't care, believing time would take care of it.

The Hudson River wasn't polluted in a day, a week, or a year. Ninety-five years ago my father enjoyed swimming in it from the Hoboken docks. It is gradual processes, like pollution, growing by small increments, which seem to baffle us. We just don't seem to get it when there is only a tiny trickle of poisons entering our air or our water.

It reminds me of a friend of mine who told this story without meaning it to be humorous. He said when he was 45 years of age he had to get a medical examination because he wanted to buy more life insurance. The insurance company sent a nurse to his office to give him a complete checkup. She was noncommittal as she checked his vital signs. He was furious at her and the world when a week later his insurance broker called to tell him the insurance company had rejected his application for added coverage. "On what grounds," he asked? "Because you are obese," answered the blunt broker. That did it. My friend blew his stack and even years later when he was relating the story to me, I could see his face redden and the veins on his neck bulge. He challenged the insurance man to a game of handball and swore he would get even with the company which had rejected him. His argument was simple and totally sincere. "I had no idea I was overweight. I weighed myself the next day and found I had gained 35 pounds since my college days. It just creeped up on me." If any of you have had a similar experience, you will know what I mean by the glitch between our perception and a reality that changes in small increments. Schools slipped slowly and we didn't notice it.

The first step in leadership is to perceive accurately your present situation and notice the difference or gap between that and what ought to be. Managers like Jerry couldn't see the gap. When Jerry became a leader, he was quick to perceive that his school and he were doing the wrong things efficiently, but missing the big picture. It was as if they were meticulously assigning deck chairs to passengers on the *Titanic*. Once he got the vision of the Year-Round School, he had the big picture. His courageous perception of the true state of his school and the gap between that and his dream drove him to implement the kind of changes that would close the gap. It happens.

Take the example of Marie, a principal. She manages a school which was once a rather good middle school. It has been slipping each year, little by little. The neighborhood has changed. The demographics of the school have changed slowly. The city has been putting less and less money into teachers' salaries, text books, air conditioning, building maintenance, etc. The better teachers have been moving away. Most of the remaining teachers are just marking time until retirement. They are polishing the brass on a sinking ship. Marie is like Jerry was before he saw the "light." Marie and Jerry were hard working principals but they had perceptual difficulties. They didn't perceive the gap between where their schools were and where they ought to be.

The first step in learning to be a leader of a school is attaining the ability or skill to see reality. Marie is a very conscientious principal. She, like Jerry, does the little things well but misses the big picture. Only a principal who has the psychological strength to step back and look at the school as objectively as possible will have the "right stuff" for bringing about change. You can't really lead without knowing what is and what ought to be. The leader-principal needs two virtues—honesty and hope.

> Leadership appears to be the art of getting others to want to do something that you, yourself, are so convinced ought to be done, that you have thrown yourself 100%, into the task of accomplishing this goal with the help of those whom you are trying to get on board.

Note that the leader wants to do something and is convinced that what he or she wants to do is the right thing to do. Only when a principal sees that something needs doing because what is, is so far from what ought to be (honesty), can the change process begin. But the change can't go on unless the leader has a vision of what ought to be and the belief that it is realizable with the help of others (hope).

HOW DOES THE LEADER LEARN WHAT OUGHT TO BE DONE?

Effective schools are run by principals, teachers, parents, students, and other stakeholders who know why the school exists. In other words, all the stakeholders in a great school share amazingly similar images or visions of what they want to achieve. They say, "We want to make this the best Middle School for the Performing Arts in New England." This vision is a force that bonds together students, teachers, and others in a common cause. It is a great thing to see in action. I have seen it in some Year-Round Schools. The school community pulling together becomes a source of energy. People work very hard, and they walk briskly, not dragging themselves around as if they were in Gulag 17. They work freely with a light in their eyes. They are people who have been inspired to want to work hard for something they really believe in. What a difference that makes in the climate of a school. The students pick it up and join in. There are fewer absentees, fewer disciplinary problems, and there is real learning taking place.

Before this can happen, however, there must be a leader with a clear vision of the Middle School for the Performing Arts and a lot of hope. No, she doesn't have a detailed blue print all ready to be implemented. She has a dream. This is the same principal, Marie, who, before she saw the light, was just a plodder. Marie has changed. She experienced a "metanoia," a fundamental shift or change of mind. The word "metanoia" helps us understand leadership. It's a Greek word that means a going beyond or changing (meta) and of the mind (nous). In a sense, all true learning is a metanoia but we reserve it for the kinds of profound learning which literally changes the way we perceive our world and ourselves in relation to it.

What happened? Marie was able to step back and look at her school objectively. She could see it in the cold light of reality (honesty). It wasn't a pleasant sight. Then Marie visited her sister in the midwest over Christmas and heard about a middle school for the performing arts in a small midwestern town named Damascus. Like Saul, Marie saw the vision on her way to Damascus and was able to share it with some of her colleagues when she returned to North Carolina. Her Middle School was a slowly sinking barge with a passable auditorium. What to do? Marie got an appointment with the superintendent and presented him with a vision—one that she and a handful of her teachers dreamed up based on the model from Damascus. In their vision, the School attracts youngsters from all over the district. They come to sing, dance, play in the orchestra, act, write scripts, do stagecraft, etc. Marie spoke up boldly to the stunned superintendent, "We think,with your support, we could turn the School into a School for the Performing Arts. A school works better when it has a unifying theme. Some of our teachers are really excited about trying a performing arts theme. Some parents like the idea also." The superintendent, well aware of the present state of affairs at the School, was delighted to see this initiative coming from Marie and some teachers he thought were charter members of the "Don't rock the boat" club. Even as I write, Marie, her teachers and a good representation of parents are in the planning stage. They are excited about inaugurating the Performing Arts School next year.

I can't wait to see how that group of teachers and that wonderful principal create a school for our times. I can see the parents and teachers building forms for the chorus. I can hear the student chorus accompanied by the Middle School orchestra singing the great song from South Pacific, "If you don't have a dream, how you gonna make a dream come true?" How fitting!

HOW DOES A PRINCIPAL INSPIRE THROUGH A SHARED VISION?

High performing organizations all have a clear vision of what they are about. They know why they exist. Their members have very similar mental images of what they want to achieve. Principals lead and inspire through a Shared Vision when they are able to fashion a vision for the whole group which is not too far removed from the personal visions of the individual members. If the principal tries to sell a vision that seems to the followers to be too far out, too difficult to achieve, too risky, the staff and parents will balk. On the other hand, if the principal's vision is too unexciting, lacking in challenge, stakeholders won't buy into it.

The way to build an effective shared vision is to find out what talents the various individuals possess, then make sure the vision is one that will ensure that the individuals have the chance to use these talents. Marie was quick to realize that many of the teachers working at the Middle School had talent in the performing arts. Three of them sang in the best chorus in the state. Two more performed in local theatre groups. The vocational education teacher had a hobby of building sets for the theater group. Four more of the staff played instruments, and the art teacher was the best asset the school had. A Shared Vision is impossible unless the personal visions of the individuals mesh to some degree with the overarching vision. Marie herself was delighted when she realized her own hobby—writing poetry—could fit nicely into a school for the Performing Arts.

Suppose we had a totally different scenario. Mike is the principal of an elementary school which is characterized by mediocrity. Mike and his wife have an all consuming interest in travel. With no children of their own they have been free to travel widely. Mike has more maps than Rand McNally. They love the *National Geographic* and plan imaginary trips to all the exotic places featured. While Mike is sharing coffee with a few of the teachers in the teachers' room, one of the middle-aged teachers said, "I'll bet we could come up with an idea that would really rejuvenate this school." Mike spilled his coffee as he turned toward the speaker. "Sure," he continued, "we could make this into an International School. Everyone is talking about Global this and Global that. It is time we started to let the kids in on the secret that the world is bigger than the United States. They will be competing for jobs not just with students from South Carolina, Virginia, and Tennessee, but from Germany, Sweden, Italy, and Poland." Now Mike and the other two teachers are really interested. Mike responded almost automatically, "We could name the corridors after different countries and have pictures of kids from those countries on the wall." Tom, the Physical Education teacher, added, "We could make the Olympics the theme for all our sports programs." "Wait a minute," said the third grade teacher, "we are situated next to a great University with a Textile School. I'll bet we have over 50 different nations represented in the student body. They could be terrific resources." The bell rang.

Two years later that mediocre elementary school is now an International School in which all the things discussed above are a reality, and that is only the tip of the iceberg. Every child in the International School is learning a second language and talking by phone to students in different countries. Mike and

26

his wife are studying Spanish after procrastinating for years. Wow!

Here we witness a Shared Vision being born. I visited that school last year. It is a winner. The staff, students, and parents love it. They show great initiative. It seems they caught the vision and now they all do the right things without being told. This is what education is all about. If you are interested in filling a pail with milk, it is not wise to sit on a stool in the middle of a field with the belief that some cow will back up to you. The principal with a Shared Vision who gets and keeps the attention of the stakeholders, finds they can go together to the cow and get more milk than they ever dreamed of. Learning is not only natural, it is invigorating. A school burning with a Shared Vision is a Learning Organization. Everyone connected with it is learning together with everyone else. They aren't just memorizing facts or dusting off old formulae, they are creating new constellations of ideas. They have joined the great conversation with the past. They live in the present with a constant eye on the future. They are alive, alert, active, thinking, dreaming, caring, growing. That is what life-long learning is all about.

Obviously, a principal cannot create a Shared Vision alone. The principal has a very important role to play. He or she must be able to state the vision in such a way that others will give it a hearing. Great principals lead well because they communicate well. They communicate well because they are able to get and keep the attention of the stakeholders. Shared Visions always take us on the road less traveled. Beaten paths are for beaten people.

The principal has to share the vision in such an exciting way that the followers will be willing to get off the beaten path. In my experience, the principal's personal investment and excitement is essential. When a principal is really excited by a vision, he or she will speak in metaphors. The language will be crisp, graphic, moving. Great principal leaders have the knack of communicating a special purpose to work that others think is ordinary.

A vision is an acute sense of the possible. It is an ideal and unique image of the future. No principal can do it without a team as we see later. The Shared Vision is so great that no one can do it alone but it is possible when the team members merge their personal visions with this overarching Shared Vision. We have seen examples of a Year-Round School, a School of the Performing Arts, and finally an International School. These are only samples of the countless visions that can transform a mediocre school into a vibrant Learning Organization. What all worthwhile Shared Visions have in common is this: they are looking forward, seeing the future, having a sense of the possible.

ALL STAKEHOLDERS ARE EMPOWERED BY THE SHARED VISION

In getting extraordinary things done in a school, everyone is important, not just the principal. Every principal I know is perfectly aware of this fact. The principals have two problems: one, how to get people to work together, and two, how to enable and empower the stakeholders so they will do the right things without being told. What a principal wants is to get people to work together by developing cooperative goals. Next the principal wants each of the team members to be enabled and empowered so they can carry out these cooperative goals.

When teachers begin to see that the Vision for the whole school is more important than their personal vision for their individual classrooms or departments, then we have a start in getting people to work together for the larger goal. This is not easy. For too many years a teacher could say to a principal, "I do a good job in my classroom and that is what I am being paid to do. You shouldn't push schoolwide projects on to me." Of late I have begun to discover that students don't quit class, they quit school. Every teacher, and that includes custodians, cafeteria workers, secretaries, assistant teachers, classroom teachers, and the principal are responsible for the learning environment of the SCHOOL. These people, plus the parents and students, are the stakeholders in the school. The trick is to get them working collaboratively and with the knowledge and skills necessary to turn a school into a genuine Learning Organization.

One thing we know for sure, the principal will not be successful in bringing about collaborative work if he or she pits one teacher or one department against another. Creating competition within the team or between team members is counterproductive. The secret is to develop cooperative goals. Team work is essential for a productive organization like a school.

I have noted that principals who develop collaboration in their schools, have a knack of showing respect for the stakeholders. Their habit of conveying warmth to the team members helps them develop cooperative goals.

One principal I respect very much told me that she discovered a way to foster collaboration. She made a point of watching for instances in which some of the stakeholders were spontaneously involved in ongoing interactions. For example, two teachers on their own were working together to make more room for the students to store their gear. The principal made a point of recognizing such interactions and praising the participants. At the teachers' meetings she regularly made a presentation she named the "Light a Candle Award." She would give a candle to stakeholders who had voluntarily carried out some project to improve school climate. Last year she gave out 78 candles.

The schools in which stakeholders have more time to associate usually show more collaboration in tasks connected with the school. As a principal you can see that the interactions carried out by teachers to improve the school climate are highly leveraged. When the students see the teachers putting themselves out to make the students' life easier, it moves them deeply and has a marvelous effect on the "esprit de corps" of the school. In fact there is a long-term payoff. Most civility is taught in a school by teachers treating each other and the students in a civil manner.

Goodlad has a rule of thumb for judging the effectiveness of principals. He claims that you can be sure you are dealing with effective principals if when asked what kind of staff they have, they respond positively, showing respect for the stakeholders. In other words, the best principals trust their people and realize all too well that their people can make or break them. Principals must first demonstrate their willingness to trust all members of their teams, before the team members can wholeheartedly put their fate in the principals' hands. A trusting principal will encourage the kind of voluntary cooperation we have been discussing.

MOST TEAMS PLAY BETTER IN HOME GAMES

We mentioned earlier that the principal needs to trust his or her staff. But how can the principal make sure that the staff he trusts is equipped to carry out the tasks expected of them? That is not cheating. If I am a leader and my fate depends on the skill and knowledge of my staff then I will be highly motivated to make that staff as strong as possible, individually and as a group. In other words, I will do all in my power to make sure that my staff is empowered.

One of the dumbest mistakes that educational administrators can make is to believe that power is a fixed sum. The dumb equation goes this way: the more powerful the leader is and the less powerful the staff members are, the better the organization will run. This way lies disaster. Or take the example of a power-mad principal who gives absolutely no delegated power to his assistant principal. What will the consequences be? You have all seen it happen.

The truth of the matter is that power is an expandable pie. People who feel powerless tend to hoard whatever shreds of power they have. They are not pleasant to work with and they usually botch the job they are doing. What principals tell me is that power is best kept by giving it away. It is a paradox. The best principals have learned a terrific lesson—give out as much power and responsibility to your staff as the staff is willing and able to accept. Then coax them into taking a little bit more. The more stakeholders realize that they can actually influence and control the school, the more they are enabled, and the more effective the school will become. Put in a slightly different way, shared power flowing from a Shared Vision results in higher job satisfaction and performance throughout the school. When we feel that we have the power to influence what is going on in our lives, we tend to perform at our best and we experience the most job satisfaction.

I have never seen a successful principal who doesn't know what I just wrote to be true and who doesn't put it into practice. It is apparent that the principal is the one who takes the largest risk, because he or she must trust an untried staff. Now we find out something about humans. They tend to act up to the level of our expectancy. If we expect little, we will get little. If we expect a lot and treat people with warmth, respect, and encouragement, they usually perform splendidly.

Once I read a story that illustrates very well the point we are making. In a nursing home, some social psychologists did this experiment. They divided the population of 80 residents into two groups, matched in age, sex, degree of illness, etc. The control group of 40 were each given a potted plant and the experimenters told them individually that the management would take responsibility for the health of the plant since they were not able to do it. The management would also choose the movie to be seen each week, and the arrangement of the furniture in the common room. The experimental group of 40 were also given individual plants, but in this case the experimenters were very clear in telling the members that they must take responsibility for the plant, and they would have to make a choice on what movie to see and how to arrange the furniture. Not only did the general health and psychological well-being of the experimental group improve, but death rates were 50% lower than they were in the control group. What happens when people are given power and responsibility is awesome. They accomplish much more than they ever thought they could.

In the Year-Round Schools I have visited in which the principals and staffs all volunteered to start their risky ventures, I observed unleashed energy that was like Niagara Falls. Most of us don't accomplish as much as we could, not because we are tired and overworked (although we may well be tired and overworked), but because we are not plugged into a Shared Vision that energizes us. Working together to realize a Shared Vision, we expect more from self and others and we usually get it.

THE PRINCIPAL IS MOST A LEADER WHEN HE OR SHE IS MODELING THE WAY

The principalship is a lonely job. There are people all around, but the principal can't really show his or her self-doubts. The good principal is the model of a social change agent. The principal sets the example and makes sure that the troops see small victories so they will keep marching to the drum beat. I guess we could say that the principal determines what basic philosophy and what set of values will be the guiding stars for the school as it steers a new course. Now we can talk about values. The personal vision of each school stakeholder and the personal vision of the principal are nothing more than the values that each espouses, integrated first into a personal and then into a shared vision. Our vision is the result of our values, and once we start to implement our vision, values come in again to determine the means we will choose to pursue the vision. So it is apparent that values are one of the most important ingredients in the life of an organization like a school. The principal's values joined with those of the other stakeholders will ultimately determine the destiny of the school.

Values comprise the things that are most important to us. They are deep-seated, pervasive standards that influence almost every aspect of our lives: our moral judgments, our responses to others, our commitments to personal and organizational goals. Even though we are not consciously aware of our values most of the time, they nevertheless give direction to the hundreds of decisions we make in our personal and professional lives. A school functions the way it does because of the values of the School Board, superintendent, central office, principal, staff, teachers, parents, students, and the local community. We don't heed opinions that are contrary to our basic values. Before principals can be models or set an example, they need to be in touch with what needs to be done. That will be a reflection of what they value most. Principals who really put children first will run a totally different school than those who give higher priority to other values: their own professional advancement, cutting costs, high ranking on tests, peace at any price, control, popularity with teachers or parents, etc.

The principal has the job of making sure that people know what the principal and the school stands for. Acting as spokesperson for the school is a function that principals should take quite seriously. The principal speaking for all the stakeholders says, "We believe that any child can learn if given the proper help." Another principal speaking for another school might say, "We believe that each child has seven different intellectual competencies and each of them is of maximum importance. So we have a philosophy which says, 'whatever we teach will be taught in such a way that all of the seven intelligences will be activated.'" Unless the principal is speaking for the whole school, none of these statements will amount to more than clanging gongs. The Shared Vision contains the values. For example, the mission statement at Washington Middle School of the Performing Arts states, "We believe that nothing that is taught could not be better taught if music and the other performing arts were somehow integrated into the process." The principal doesn't have to run around the school checking to see that music and other art forms are being integrated into all aspects of the curriculum. Rather, the principal can assume that every stakeholder is always trying to come up with more and better ways to touch each child's competencies through the performing arts. While visions refer to the future and to what the school ought to be doing, values refer to the means (the how) by which these ends can be best achieved.

Shared values make all the difference in the world. The principal's values serve as the standards for others about what is important in the school. When individual values and school values are synchronized, a tremendous amount of raw energy is unleashed. The principal models not by trying to find better values, but by being faithful to the values professed in the Shared Vision. It is not easy to do. There is a big difference between "espoused values," what we say we believe, and "values in use," those that we actually use. To say in our school we take into consideration multicultural differences and to really do it are two different things. The good principals lead by example.

JOHN D. ROCKEFELLER'S CREED

Besides a mission statement, each school should have a written creed. The school can't have a written vision because the vision is into the future and is always changing. But a school could and should have a creed. One very cold night in February, a few years ago, my wife and I stopped at Rockefeller

Center to watch the people ice skating on the outdoor rink. It was very cold and my hands were freezing. Despite the cold, I took time out to write down what I read on a plaque just in front of the ice rink. What I copied that cold night was John D. Rockefeller's creed, one of the finest I have ever seen. By today's standards, it seems old-fashioned, and it is certainly sexist, but despite these drawbacks it does offer food for reflection. We should have it displayed in the school for all to see:

I believe in the supreme worth of the individual and his right to life, liberty and the pursuit of happiness.

I believe that every right implies a responsibility; every opportunity, an obligation; every possession, a duty.

I believe that the law was made for man and not man for the law; that government is the servant of the people and not their master.

I believe in the dignity of labor, whether with head or hand; that the world owes no man a living, but that it owes every man an opportunity to make a living.

I believe that thrift is essential to well ordered living and that economy is a prime requisite of a sound financial structure, whether in government, business, or personal affairs.

I believe that truth and justice are fundamental to an enduring social order.

I believe in the sacredness of a promise, that a man's word should be as good as his bond; that character—not wealth or power or position—is of supreme worth.

I believe that the rendering of useful service is the common duty of mankind and that only; in the purifying fire of sacrifice is the dross of selfishness consumed and the greatness of the human soul set free.

I believe in an all-wise and all loving God, named by whatever name, and that the individual's highest fulfillment, greatest happiness, and widest usefulness are found in living in harmony with His will.

A FORMULA TO HELP PRINCIPALS FOR OUR CHANGING SCHOOLS

In the study made by the National Policy Board for Educational Administrators, we can find a formula which sums up what we have been saying. *In Principals For Our Changing Schools*, the authors offer a process model that is clear and very practical.

> "Principals give their schools purpose and direction by developing a shared strategic vision, shaping school culture and values, and formulating school improvement efforts. Principals do not perform these tasks in isolation, but rather serve as facilitators, eliciting the involvement of the stakeholders and ensuring that such efforts are carried out." (4)

When the authors break down the functions of the principals in school renewal they go into more detail. In order for a principal to inculcate school culture and values, he or she must have the following knowledge and skills.

◆ The principal must have a well-developed educational philosophy.

◆ The principal must have high expectations of all the stakeholders. If there is one thing we can say with certainty it is this: in school renewal the principal never gets more than he or she expected. They often get less. Put more positively, the higher the expectations the principal places on the stakeholders, the greater the school renewal.

◆ The principal must understand the school culture. This may sound simplistic but it isn't. I have met many principals who were totally oblivious of the culture in their school. Jerry knew where every paperclip was but he didn't have a clue about the overall culture of his school. To understand the culture, the principal has to spend a lot of time listening to the students, parents, and teachers.

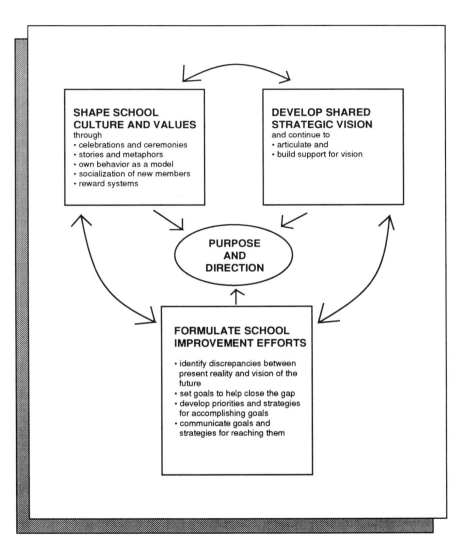

**SHAPE SCHOOL
CULTURE AND VALUES**
through
• celebrations and ceremonies
• stories and metaphors
• own behavior as a model
• socialization of new members
• reward systems

**DEVELOP SHARED
STRATEGIC VISION**
and continue to
• articulate and
• build support for vision

*PURPOSE
AND
DIRECTION*

**FORMULATE SCHOOL
IMPROVEMENT EFFORTS**

• identify discrepancies between
present reality and vision of the
future
• set goals to help close the gap
• develop priorities and strategies
for accomplishing goals
• communicate goals and
strategies for reaching them

◆ The principal must be perceptive, not missing a trick as far as school rituals and behaviors are concerned. Sharp principals frequently ask questions such as, "What do people consider to be significant events within the school?" "How is conflict handled?" "Who are the school's recognized heroes and villains?" "What behaviors are rewarded, which ones punished?" We will discuss this more fully in the next chapter, "Knowing What is What."

◆ Successful principals know how to build consensus. They have the skills to communicate a shared understanding of cultural values. It would be hard to exaggerate the importance of communication skills for the principals. We will refer often to this skill in later chapters. At the Principals' Executive Program we put a lot of stress on written and oral communication skills.

◆ The principal must reflect school culture in his or her behavior. How often have I visited a school and seen posters on the walls touting civility only to be met by a school secretary who is brusque, impersonal, and totally lacking in social skills. Unfortunately, I know immediately that the principal will reflect the same negative school culture. What keeps me going is the number of principals I meet who truly reflect a positive school culture. They are out in the rain meeting the buses and hugging the elementary school children, yet they have time for you and treat you like a friend.

◆ As we said previously, the principals who are going to change schools for the better have the great gift of integrity. Their "espoused values" closely mirror their "values in use." The principal symbolically communicates the values of the school. In a civil school, the principal is civility personified.

◆ The successful principal has the ability to align the reward system with the school's values. They have the knack of catching people doing something right and celebrating the event. A principal who cares about the cleanliness of her school building will stop and praise a student who is picking up trash from the cafeteria floor to deposit it in the wastebasket. The principal of a school with high academic standards will be most alert in spotting and rewarding students who are striving for academic excellence.

To close this chapter, I will share with you an exercise from *Principals For Our Changing Schools*. It is called Visioning. The purpose is to give you some real experience in visioning. Close your eyes and try to imagine a school that doesn't yet exist. It is your vision of the ideal school. You imagine that you have a staff that will buy into this vision and be willing to throw themselves wholeheartedly into making it a reality. Now ask yourself these questions:

◆ What do you see around you in the school of your dreams? What sounds do you hear? What are you doing? How are you feeling?

◆ Join a meeting of teachers, what do you see occurring? How are the teachers interacting? What do you see, hear, feel? How has this changed from before?

◆ Walk around the building. What do you see happening?

◆ Notice any interaction between a teacher and a student. What occurs?

◆ Talk to a parent. What are you discussing? What is the parent saying? How is it different from before? (5)

SUMMATION

In this chapter, I discussed the important leadership role principals play in site-based management. Helping to form and share the vision, empowering stakeholders, and modeling the way, principals become the key players in changing schools into Learning Organizations.

In his masterful study, *A Place Called School,* John I. Goodlad says, in so many words, that educational renewal must take place in a school by school process. More importantly, the success of site renewal is greatly dependent upon the degree to which the principal and other stakeholders have the data required to build a useful agenda. In other words, school renewal must start with knowing what is what in the school. Our next chapter will deal with what the National Policy Board calls" Information Collection."

QUESTIONS FOR REFLECTION

1. In Chapter 2 I offer a definition of leadership. After reading it over again and reflecting on it, see if you can find any of the following ideas hidden in it: Shared Vision, Team Learning, Motivation, Delegation, Commitment, Values, Communication?

2. In times of crisis, we often find ordinary people placed in positions of authority who seem to rise to the challenge and become extraordinary leaders. Why is this the case?

3. What would you have to say about the superintendent who gave such a mixed review on his principal, Jerry? When he sent Jerry to the Principals' Executive Program, he said he hoped the staff would light a fire under Jerry. Can the PEP staff accomplish this goal? How?

4. Compare the definition of leadership I offered in this chapter with the one I quoted from *Principals For Our Changing Schools.* How are they the same ? How are they different?

5. How did Marie's visit to her sister in the Midwest have such a profound influence on her, and eventually on her school? Do you believe in sudden life changes?

6. High performing organizations are characterized by clear vision? How do they get to know exactly what they are about?

7. How can you explain the fact that all stakeholders are actually empowered by the Shared Vision? Neither Marie nor Mike were reluctant to share power with their stakeholders. According to Goodlad's litmus test, Marie and Mike were good principals because they had great respect for their staffs and from their staffs.

8. The more school stakeholders realize that they can actually exert real influence and have some control over where the school is going, the more enabled and energized they become and the more effective the school becomes. When we feel we have some power to influence what is going on in our lives we feel a lot more job satisfaction. Take those two statements and state them in a negative form. Reflect for a few moments, and then discuss how different the results become.

10. Would you want your own children to be exposed to John D. Rockefeller's Creed? Why? Why not?

3

KNOWING WHAT IS WHAT

When one shuts one eye, one does not hear everything.
Swiss proverb
We don't know one millionth of one percent about anything.
Thomas Edison

When we talk we can only say something that we already know. When we listen we may learn what someone else knows. This chapter is concerned with the duty the principal has to collect the information necessary to make good decisions. There are many ways of collecting and handling information. I will give priority to the art of probing because I think it is a skill that is essential to learning from and about others.

Before we start getting into skills of listening and learning that characterize a principal adept at information collecting, we should clarify what information itself is. One of the most striking signs of our times is the fact that people who are supposed to be experts in various fields can no longer deal with the urgent problems that have arisen in their area of expertise. Economists are unable to understand inflation, oncologists are totally confused about the causes of cancer, educators cannot explain why the schools turn out so many students ill

41

equipped to function in the work world, psychiatrists are still mystified by schizophrenia, police are helpless in the face of rising crime, and the list goes on. The river of wisdom has now split off into so many specialized rivulets that it is almost impossible to find people who think about and have understanding of the whole situation. Only an observant and perceptive principal can understand the whole school. The principal must be able to see the whole picture, use common sense, and gather information wherever and whenever he can. Most principals spend too little time on this.

If this is the case, what can a principal of a school do? He or she cannot get clear answers from the experts. The experts have all specialized to such a point that none of them see the school as the principal does—a living, pulsating organism with its own tendencies to bolt this way and that. The principal sees the school as a system, and the school in terms of relationships and integration.

The systems approach emphasizes basic principles of organization. Every school is a whole whose structure arises from the interactions and interdependence of their parts. If one set of interactions goes off, the whole school is affected. Let's take a simple example, the heating system stops functioning at 10:15AM on Monday, February 4. The repair men come and say they need parts that must be sent from a supply warehouse 4 hours away. The school cannot be heated for the rest of the day or by the next morning. Now tell me some part of the school that is not affected by this problem. Someone will say, "that is obvious, whenever a mechanical function like that goes off, the whole school is affected. Give us an example that has nothing to do with heating, lighting, etc."

John I. Goodlad in his book, *A Place Called School*, lists what he calls the "commonplaces of schooling." I will call them the elements that make up a school but which cannot stand alone. Each element should be viewed from the perspectives of students, teachers, and parents and other stakeholders. The commonplaces are as follows: teaching practices, content or subject matter, instructional materials, physical environment, activities, human resources, evaluation, time, organization, communication, decisionmaking, leadership, expectations, issues and problems, controls or restraints.

Suppose any one of these commonplaces is drastically changed, what will happen to all the others? No principal with more than 1 year of experience will even hesitate to give the answer: "When one of these goes off, the whole school goes off." Take the last one—controls and restraints. We are seeing this, unfortunately, in our school today. When middle school students bring loaded guns to school, we know what happens to teaching, learning, extracurricular activities, communication, physical environment, etc. We know the effect it has on students, teachers, and parents. Take human resources as another example. What happens when a large number of teachers miss many days of school, even with quite legitimate excuses? Harassed principals have countless stories to tell about what happens to the other commonplaces when you have too many substitute teachers working in the school on the same day.

There is an old joke about a giraffe in which a group of people are trying to figure out why this peculiar animal has such an elongated neck. Finally, one of the wags says, "It's probably because the giraffe was designed by a committee and the member in charge of necks had too much clout." I've seen the same thing happen in schools where the English teachers had too much power, or the coach, cafeteria lady, or assistant principal reigned supreme. A school is a complex living organism like a human person. The fragile balance can easily be fractured, so the principal must know at all times how the various elements are functioning together, and how they can grow and adjust to the changing environment. Too much parental intervention may be deleterious, too little may be disastrous.

WHAT JOHN I. GOODLAD FOUND

I have always found the book, *A Place Called School,* invaluable in my work with school principals. John I. Goodlad gives us the best picture of schools in America today. It is a masterful study in which he applies the 15 commonplaces of schooling to 38 schools. He and his team gathered information from 17,163 students, 8,624 parents, and 1,350 teachers. Because he collected such a great amount of material, he couldn't use it without analyzing it and presenting it in a manageable format. This is something each principal has to learn to do with the information collected in his or her school. Goodlad solves his problem by identifying a number of *themes* which tell us a lot about schools and schooling. Each of his *themes,* which I will share with you, derives its qualities from the way several related commonplaces manifest themselves, as perceived by the several groups of respondents and observers.

The first *theme* is *school functions.* He found that schools perform many different functions—from babysitting to job preparation and intellectual development. Unfortunately, Goodlad found with his 38 schools that although they should almost exclusively emphasize their educational function, they do not.

The second *theme* refers to the school's *relevance in the lives of its students.* Students are the schools primary clients, but they don't go to school seeking educational services in the way they go to the doctor for health services. They go to school as part of growing up. They don't have clear, common purposes for being in school. This is one of the biggest problems every principal faces, how can we make school-based learning meaningful, to say nothing of compelling or exciting. Goodlad wonders what schools are doing to recognize changes in the values of the young. Principals must consistently seek to know how they can make their schools more relevant to the lives of the boys and girls who attend them. When my father used to ask me every night, "What did you learn in school today?," I, as a third grader, would answer, "Nothing." This seemed to infuriate him, and I really wished there was something else I could have said. My problem was that nothing I had learned in school that day seemed to have any relevance to me or my father. If only there had been a clearer connection between what I was learning in school and what was happening at home, my father would have been less infuriated and I would have remembered the material better.

The third *theme* concerns itself with *how teachers teach.* We will devote a large part of Chapter 9 precisely to this theme. To my way of thinking it is the most important of all the themes.

The fourth *theme* is *the circumstances surrounding teaching.* Circumstances in a school that positively affect teachers can't help but benefit students. Unfortunately, the contrary is also true. If teachers are unhappy in their workplace situations, they will not do a good job teaching the students. So it stands to reason that if we want to improve a school, we should spend a lot more time and effort enhancing the working conditions for the teachers. We will spend a considerable amount of time on this subject later in the book.

The fifth *theme* is concerned with the array of activities, materials, and tests constituting the curriculum. I will treat this matter at length in Chapters 10.

The sixth *theme* is the *distribution of resources for learning*. The most important of these is *time*. In collecting information about a school, a principal and the other stakeholders would accomplish something great if they just tried to conduct a real study of the use of classroom and school time. According to Goodlad, only about 70% of classroom time is utilized for instruction. The use of time could and should be a major concern to each principal. In order to control and improve the use of time we have to get some idea of how it is presently being spent.

The seventh *theme* is *equity*. There is concern in public schools for how justly the resources for learning are distributed. For instance, the use of tracking may well be an unjust way of distributing these resources. In too many instances, the most successful students get the best teachers and the less successful students are taught by the least skilled teachers. The great disparity between the "haves" and the "have nots," even in the same school system, has led some to question whether we are offering equal access to quality education.

The eighth *theme* is often referred to as *the hidden curriculum* Prescinding from what schools explicitly teach such as reading, writing, and figuring, they also teach a great deal implicitly. It reminds me of the old song, "It ain't what you do, it's the way how you do it." In presenting the explicit curriculum, a school can either stress the acquiring of facts or the solving of problems. Much is implicitly taught by the rules of a school and the physical setting in which teaching and learning take place. An example: suppose you are a 10 year old in fourth grade and you begin to realize that the school is the only non-air conditioned place in which you spend a significant amount of time. Your home, the Y, the movie theatre, the mall, your parents' car, are all air conditioned. Only school is a hot box. What does that tell the 10 year old about the importance of learning in school? What does it say about the comfort of teachers and, hence, the importance of teaching in this world? For sure, it says to the fourth grader (in the hidden curriculum) school is not as important as the mall, and nowhere near as much fun. A second example: what happens to learning when a seventh grader begins to realize that the school is the only place that features one-on-one competitiveness in learning? Her parents tells her about work teams and cooperative learning in their jobs. She wonders why school pits students against each other, while in the work world the ideal is teamwork.

In collecting information, the principal and stakeholders have a difficult task. They must assess the hidden curriculum as well as they do the more explicit one, sent down from the central office. Schools implicitly teach values and, not surprisingly, these values are often assimilated better by the students than are the more explicit teachings. The explicit curriculum reflects our "espoused values;" the hidden curriculum is a reflection of our "values in use."

The ninth *theme* is *satisfaction as a criterion of school quality.* In his Chapter 8, in *A Place Called School,* John I. Goodlad presents his findings on the level of satisfaction for the 38 schools studied. He measures principals', students', parents', and teachers' satisfaction levels. This chapter is a gold mine for any principal who seriously wants to improve his or her school. Goodlad's conclusion is simple but revolutionary. He tells us that the composite satisfaction of principal, teachers, students, and parents constitutes a significant indication of a school's quality, including achievement. If the main stakeholders express satisfaction over their school, it is in all probability a quality school.

In collecting information, one of the first things a manufacturer does is try to measure customers' satisfaction with the product he makes. Service organizations also try to measure their customers' satisfaction level. It is surprising that we waited so long to discover this in schools, yet it's understandable. Why should principals have tried to measure the levels of satisfaction among school stakeholders at a time when they had no authority or autonomy to do anything about a lack of satisfaction? Now, with site management, the situation has changed. Principals need to be very sensitive to the levels of satisfaction expressed by students, teachers, and parents on all the commonplaces we outlined earlier. Goodlad did this for the 38 schools he studied. Each principal with the help of stakeholders should be doing this regularly at the site level.

The tenth *theme is the need for data.* It is a rare school these days which possesses the information needed by its stakeholders to set, with some confidence, an agenda for school improvement. Very few principals or teachers know the distribution of curricular emphases as experienced by any given student. They don't know the proportion of students in academic programs who also enrolled in vocational education classes. Few teachers can speak with any confidence about how the students view the curriculum. The teachers can't tell you whether or not the curriculum of students in their home room is well-balanced.

After years of research, Goodlad passes on to us two insights which are profound. First, we must believe that the school is the unit for improvement. It can't be done from above. It can't be done by well-meaning people who are far removed from the smell of the chalk. His second insight is more of a surprise. He tells us that our schools will get better and have continuing good health only to the degree that a significant proportion of our citizens, not just parents, care about them. He believes that caring for our schools hit the skids in the 1970s.

One of the best ways we can make sure that school improvement takes place at the site level, and that a wider slice of the public begins to care again about what happens to our public schools is for all the stakeholders to do whatever they can to collect the necessary information.

AVOID COLLECTING EVERYTHING COLLECTIBLE

Maybe this is an unnecessary caveat, but I would hate to see individual schools do what so many school systems and government agencies do—collect for the sake of collecting. They collect data simply because it is there, and then fail to use it for any constructive purpose. Too many unnecessary forms are presently choking the schools. These meaningless forms steal educators' time and keep teachers from teaching and principals from being more creative. What I am suggesting, as far as the collection of information, is not like that at all. It is site-based and practical.

Hugh Troy, an artist and writer who was drafted into the army during World War II, was sent as a company clerk to a southern Army camp that was far from busy. The flow of paperwork however was growing as the real activity dwindled. This started to drive Hugh crazy. Reports, reports, and more reports in trivial detail were mandated by the Pentagon.

One day Troy, the practical joker, devised a special report form and had it mimeographed. It was regarding the number of flies trapped during each 24-hour period on the 20 flypaper ribbons that hung in the mess hall. His report included a sketch plan of the mess hall showing the location of each ribbon of flypaper in relation to entrances, tables, lights, windows, and kitchen. Each ribbon was identified by a code number. Troy's first flypaper report showed that during a 24-hour period, Flypaper Ribbon X-5 trapped and retained 49 flies. Ribbon Y-2 did even better with 63 flies. And so on. He sent the report off to the Pentagon in triplicate. Each succeeding day he sent another report.

About a week after Hugh had started sending in his first flypaper reports, two fellow soldier-clerks called on him from nearby camps. They asked him if he had been getting the devil from Washington about some goofy flypaper reports.

"Why, no," said Hugh.

"It's about a daily report on flypaper in the mess halls," said the visitors. "We've been getting Pentagon queries, wanting to know why we haven't been sending them in."

"Oh," said Hugh. " I send mine in every day."

They protested that nobody had told them about any flypaper reports, so Troy gave them copies of his mimeographed form. From that day on every bundle that went to the Pentagon included a current census of dead flies. Hugh thinks it's possible that the daily flypaper report became standard Army procedure. For all we know, some Army clerk may be counting dead flies and filling out his report as we speak. This kind of nonsensical collecting of information is not what we have in mind. We do too much of that already in the government and the schools.

PRINCIPALS FOR OUR CHANGING SCHOOLS NEED TO LEARN HOW TO PROBE

Of course principals don't have to do a census on dead flies but they do need to find out what the students, teachers, and parents think and feel concerning the 15 commonplaces we alluded to earlier. How would you set about educing this information? How would you get the stakeholders to open up and talk about what they know, think, and feel about themselves and their schools? My suggestion is Probing. A principal who has this skill will have a great advantage in our changing schools. Probing has a wonderful effect. It gets people to be more receptive to new ideas and visions. As we talk about ourselves and our ideas, we become less defensive about considering new projects and programs.

To understand what probing is we have to ask ourselves what a probe is. A probe is a technique for finding out what somebody knows, thinks, or feels. Doctors and dentists use probes—thin metal instruments to explore wounds, cavities, or root canals. Happily, the probes school principals use are much less painful or threatening. Principals' probes are verbal tools used to explore minds and hearts. It is impossible for a principal to lead a school into renewal unless he or she knows what the stakeholders really know, feel, and think about themselves and their relations with the school. *The whole process of school renewal rests on the ability of the principal to find out what the administrators, teachers, students, parents, and others impacted by the school know, think, and feel about the institution as it presently exists.* This is the way principals learn to know "what is what."

Now in the second wave of educational reform the emphasis is on the individual school renewing itself with the help of many outside groups. This is the message Goodlad is preaching. We can renew the school system, school by school, if two things happen. First, the stakeholders in each school must collect the information needed to devise a solid renewal plan which takes into account the input of those most affected.

Second, knowledge or, as some call it, intelligence, should be shared with stakeholders, school boards, central offices, legislative committees, business school coalitions, etc.

Think of a school as an organism or even a living person, one who starts out young and gradually matures and ages. A newly opened school is very much like a very young child. A young child is a model of openness to new experiences—receptive, curious, eager, unafraid, willing to try anything, and above all uninhibited by fixed attitudes and habits. I have watched three brand new Year-Round Schools as they began their respective journeys. They were flexible, ready to learn, and brimming with joyful exuberance.

As persons and schools get older and more mature, they have to give up some of these priceless qualities. Inevitably, youths and schools, with the passage of time, acquire new habits, attitudes, opinions. They become more closed and guarded. This is not altogether bad news. The youths are now picking up good coping skills to manage routine changes in the environment. Their policies and procedures enable them to do things more quickly and without as much conscious choosing. Perhaps, if they stayed as open and fearless as a child, they might not be able to withstand "the slings and arrows of outrageous fortune."

However, these advantages only come at a price. Each time a young person or a school acquires another habit or routine, it becomes a little less receptive to new ways of thinking and acting. Schools, like young persons, begin to get set in their ways. While getting more competent to function in the environment, the young person or school trades this for a lessening capacity to make rapid changes when situations demand it. Here is the human predicament: we can't remain flexible and receptive like an infant all the rest of our lives or we won't get mature and hardened enough to cope with the environment. On the other hand, if the school or the young person gets too fixed in habits, attitudes, and opinions, both will be seriously hampered when the environment demands flexibility. We are presently at a stage in school renewal when we must be able to show flexibility and a readiness to try new experiments.

The principals and stakeholders are called upon to examine the encrustations (defenses) which accrued as the school battled past environmental onslaughts. Some people refer to encrustations or defenses as "sacred cows." It is difficult to discover and cut away these "hardenings" because they were, at one time, the means by which we were saved. Unfortunately, these "hardenings" can interfere with the principal's and other stakeholders' perception of the present condition of the school. Without this clearer perception the principal and stakeholders will find it impossible to remap and redirect the life of the school.

A school whose maturing consists simply of acquiring more firmly established ways of doing things is headed for decay. An efficient school can rot and decay precisely because it is doing the wrong things exceptionally well. *All organisms tend toward self-preservation through conformism.* It is easy to lose sight of the fact that schools exist for the good of the students. Sometimes the stakeholders in a decaying school will reach a point where they actually consider sacrificing the students for the sake of the school. To avoid such absurdity, the principal and stake-holders need to continuously collect information about the school as it is today.

We don't have to look far to come up with some examples of changes in the environment which seriously impact the way schools are run. Are our school children in the middle- and late-90's very much like children in the 50's? It doesn't take much probing to discover that our youth culture in the 90's is powerfully preoccupied with itself; with brand name clothes; with instant gratification; with TV channel zapping; with sexually and violently tinged rap, song, and dance .

If the principal and other stakeholders collect information about the work world for which they are preparing their students, they are in for some major surprises. Today's businesses judge employees on their ability to work on teams. Japanese and German schools aim at developing a cooperative spirit among the students. This takes precedence over individual competitiveness. Many companies want workers who can adapt to significant changes inside and outside their chosen careers. To produce that kind of student, schools will have to overhaul the system that sorts children, rather than encourages each to reach his or her potential. A former president of three major universities, now in retirement, claims that Educational bureaucrats—from elementary schools to universities—generally are reluctant to make these kinds of changes which threaten their job security.

IS THERE NO HOPE? OF COURSE THERE IS. ENTER PROBING!

A school can age and mature without decay only if it becomes a system in which there is an easy flow of information. Such a school is really a community of learners in which all the units are interdependent and communicate with each other continuously. In this kind of school, continuous innovation can occur. This ability of a person or organization (school) to mature without losing flexibility, and the capacity to adjust to change, demands keen perception, a consciousness of what is happening inside and outside the school, and an effective communication network. We could learn about this by studying the telephone network, middle school students engage in every night after school. Believe me, no shred of information is missed by this vast and efficient network. No school can be in a continually renewing mode unless the school stakeholders know how to probe with skill.

Probing has two main functions. First, it helps investigate what is going on in other peoples' minds and hearts. It is a data-gathering tool used to discover what the school community members know about various school goals and practices. It seeks to find out how these stakeholders evaluate the goals, practices, and procedures. Most importantly, probing aims at finding out what the stakeholders like or dislike, find helpful or less than helpful. In order to renew a school the principal has to continually probe these 15 commonplaces. *It is what is unknown about a school that impedes its renewal.*

The second main function of probing is to increase the receptivity of the stakeholders in the school. It is aimed at stimulating activity and involvement. Implicit is the belief that if we really probe another person—ask open-ended questions— this shows our interest. We really care about what the student, parent, or teacher knows, thinks, and feels. People generally respond favorably to being consulted about situations that directly affect them. Students blossom when they are included in the planning and decisionmaking. So do teachers and parents. Remember how justifiably irked you were as a principal when the assistant superintendent for middle schools made changes in your school's curriculum and scheduling without requesting your input and that of your teachers?

SOCRATES WAS THE PROBER PAR EXCELLENCE

Socrates was the teacher who best exemplified the art of probing. His school was called the Peripatetic School because Socrates and his students walked in the Agora at Athens. As they walked, Socrates probed the students for their knowledge and understanding. He really believed that edu-cation was a process of educing, leading out, midwifing the concepts of the students. Socrates believed the students knew a lot more than they thought they did, and he would probe to help them express their concepts. Socrates believed that probing was the quintessential tool for teaching. It's the most essential tool for school renewal also.

It isn't usually factual knowledge we are after in probing. It is the evaluative and the emotional. When we probe we are trying to get the person to give his or her opinion or estimate of some person, place, thing, event, organization, method, or procedure. Ask an elementary school student what she likes most and least about school, and what she would change if she could. You will come up with some interesting observations. If you follow-up on one or more of these offerings you will begin to see the commonplaces of schooling through a consumer's eyes.

Here is an interesting example of probing. A group of fifth graders were used by a wise principal as a "focus group." The principal put them at ease, served lemonade and cookies, and asked them to tell her what was the most fun in school. Slowly it became apparent that the randomly chosen group had a lot in common. They offered, one by one, rather well-packaged responses. "We like music, arts and crafts, physical education, and any assignment that let's us work together and talk and listen to music while we work. We like longer times to do some of the class work. We like to have more time to socialize between class periods." This was only the beginning. When the principal probed more deeply she found out why they liked these activities so much. They weren't asking for less work, rather for more variety in the use of head, hands, and heart.

When I question students about their apathy in school, they tell me the school is concerned with subjects and activities that don't seem to have any connection with their everyday lives. What does concern students? The Corporation for Public Broadcasting polled a wide sample of students 6 to 17 years of age and found the following.

◆ Given a choice between a phone or a TV in their rooms, the TV wins hands down
◆ 58% worry about making money
◆ 56% worry about pollution and the environment
◆ 48% worry about getting aids
◆ 46% worry about getting into college
◆ 44% worry about having to fight in a war
◆ The most popular after school activities included:
  • Watching TV (79%)
  • Talking on the phone (49%)
  • Doing chores (46%)
  • Sports (27%)

Why did the Corporation for Public Broadcasting have to find these things out? I would expect that in any school the stakeholders would know what the students in their classes worry about and find most attractive. A principal I know encourages all middle school teachers to ride the bus periodically with their students in order to get a feel for the neighborhoods they come from. There are countless ways to collect information about a school, and probing is one of the better ones.

SEEING A SCHOOL AS A SYSTEM HELPS IN COLLECTING INFORMATION

The schema found in *Principals for Our Changing Schools* (6) tells us to think about a school as a system. A holistic system has numerous subsystems that work together to accomplish goals and objectives, as exemplified in schools with highly interactive and interdependent subsystems.

According to systems theory, your school capitalizes on many different "inputs" (*e.g.*, children, teachers, laws, finances, community attitudes, the media, etc.). It then "transforms" these inputs (through teaching, curriculum, leadership, etc.) into "outcomes" (student achievements, parental satisfaction, a positive school climate, etc.). When you, as the principal, with the help of the other stakeholders, consider what information is needed in order to run the school well, you can look at the three subsystems: inputs or resources, transformation process or strategies, and finally the outcomes. If you take the 15 commonplaces and the three perspectives and apply them to these three subsystems, you will then have a systemic view of the school and know where the critical sources of information are located.

Moreover your school is contained in a larger environment. If your school has a good amount of interaction with its external environment: the neighborhood, business groups, government agencies, civic groups, etc., it is considered an "open" system. It also means that there is a flow of information within the school and back and forth to the outer environment. If we, as school people, are going to get others to "care" more about the plight of public schools, we will have to seek more information from without and share more information with the larger environment. "Principals, who lead their schools with an open system approach, will find readily available the types and sources of information they need in order to accomplish specific tasks." (7) In the next section we will focus on the process of collecting information.

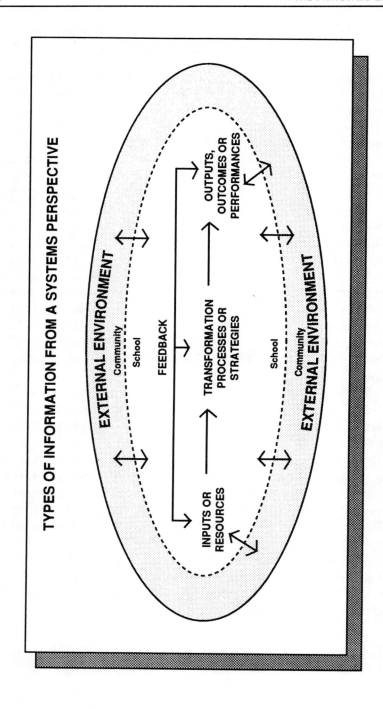

TYPES OF INFORMATION FROM A SYSTEMS PERSPECTIVE

Once you, as a principal, identify a need for information, you must determine the type of information you must collect. A good information system should give you ready access to information in three areas: resources, strategies, and performance. As you focus your attention on inputs, transformations, and outputs, you will decide what information you need and how best to collect it.

A PROCESS MODEL FOR COLLECTING SCHOOL INFORMATION

When the National Policy Board was trying to determine what knowledge and skills principals should have, they asked the practicing principals for their ideas. The process model I will now share with you was derived from the responses of practicing principals. This is what your fellow principals think is a good way to go about collecting information. The model has eight distinct steps, each of which requires specific knowledge, skills, and behaviors.

STEP 1   HOW TO DETERMINE WHAT INFORMATION IS NEEDED

Having read the story about Hugh Troy and the famous "Flypaper Reports," it is clear that we don't want to burden principals with collecting unnecessary information which will disappear in a black hole and never be used for any constructive purpose. Although many people don't realize it, the collecting of information costs money. If we could cut the time presently spent by principals and teachers on the collection of useless information, we would do a great service to the educational system. Let's agree principals don't collect any information unless they and their stakeholders determine there is a reason for collecting it. A good way to determine this will be to use the systems model. Is more information needed about the inputs, process, or incomes? What specifically do we need to know about the incoming students, new teachers, funds available, etc. How much time do the third grade teachers spend on instruction? Is it better than 70%? If not, why not? Are there too many announcements in all the classes? Ask the teachers. Ask the students what they remember about the announcements.

STEP 2 HOW TO SELECT APPROPRIATE SOURCES OF INFORMATION

One of the best ways to select appropriate sources of information is to check those sources that have been most reliable in the past. Ask the stakeholders if they can come up with some new sources of information that we haven't thought of until now. Suppose we are curious about absenteeism. Could merchants at the nearby mall give us any pertinent information? Do they see school age children in the mall during school hours? Where do they hang out? The Chamber of Commerce is another great source of information. So are real estate people.

STEP 3 WHAT ARE THE BEST STRATEGIES OR TOOLS FOR COLLECTING INFORMATION

Just as there are many ways to skin a cat, so there are many strategies for collecting information. Each strategy has its own strengths and limitations. One of the first rules of thumb I have used in my career is to follow-up any paper responses with oral exchange. For years, my wife and I tested executives and applicants for Police and Fire Departments. We always used a wide battery of tests with the belief that when one test was corroborated by data from others, the results probably had some merit. After the tests were administered by my wife, I would spend from 1 to 2 hours doing an in-depth interview with each applicant. After my wife scored the tests, I would make my observations to her on each applicant, and she would check to see if my observations were confirmed or contradicted by the test results.

I would not want to leave you with the impression that the collecting of information is something that should be left only to professional psychologists or statisticians. Every principal and every teacher should spend a large amount of their time collecting information by asking the kinds of questions that elicit rich material. It is a part of good human conversation.

STEP 4 HOW TO COLLECT OR GATHER THE INFORMATION

Not only do principals need to be able to gather information from a wide variety of sources, they should also train the teachers and other staff members to be partners in this information collection process. The National Policy Board advises principals to administer tests and measurements appropriately and to follow the administrative procedures with great care.

STEP 5 HOW TO ORGANIZE THE INFORMATION

Collected material is worthless to the principal if it is disorganized or unmanageable. Each of you, I am sure, has a system of classifying which suits your personality and temperament. There is no one right way of organizing material. There is, however, an infallible test which proves whether your system is a good or bad one. If you can find the material quickly and easily your system of classification is working for you.

STEP 6 HOW TO ANALYZE THE INFORMATION

The most important point I can make here is to tell you that you can analyze information in many ways. Although statistics are very helpful in analyzing such information, they are not, by any means, the only way. The reason I add this caveat is rather simple. Many of us in graduate school found statistics class anything but easy. I got so frightened by my first course, I came close to throwing in the towel and quitting the program. I wish central office reached out to help principals use basic statistical methods in a practical way. Principals are interested in finding out as much as they can about their own school, and statistics used correctly could be a great help to them.

One excellent way to analyze information collected is to compare it across classifications or categories by contrasting responses of different groups and subgroups to see if you can spot significant differences between them. An examination of Goodlad's *A Place Called School*, will give you countless models of the way he did just that, by comparing the 38 schools on a variety of variables. For instance, he came up with the nine most and the nine least satisfactory schools, and then found that the most satisfactory schools tended to be the ones in which the principal and other stakeholders were in the process of renewal. Also, the most satisfactory schools outscored the others on these key indices: perceived curriculum relevance, academic ambience, lack of fear and violence, quality of educational program, lack of academic apathy. Notice how many are academic in nature. Good schools feature teaching and learning of a high quality.

STEP 7 HOW TO SUMMARIZE AND DESCRIBE THE INFORMATION

No matter whether you have quantitative information in statistical form or qualitative information in anecdotal form, you still have to summarize and describe the information before you can present it to others. Goodlad took his data and sorted it around the 15 commonplaces and the three perspectives: parents, students, teachers. This produced several very large data sourcebooks which he was able to organize around the 10 themes: school function; relevance; how teachers teach; circumstances surrounding teaching; the array of activities, materials, and tests constituting the curriculum; the distribution of resources for learning; equity; hidden curriculum; satisfaction; need for more data. This could serve as a good model for principals.

STEP 8 HOW TO PRESENT THE INFORMATION TO THOSE WHO HAVE A NEED TO KNOW

Principals must be able to present information in a logical, appropriate, and interesting manner. Nothing is duller than a diet of unseasoned statistics. What most principals tell me is that the hardest job is to select the specific information that will be most relevant to the hearer, and to present it in an interesting way. We could all improve on those communication skills.

SUMMATION

In this chapter we talked about knowing "what is what." In the next chapter we will discuss "Fixing What Is Broken." One of the most difficult things for principals is to fix things if they don't know they are broken. However, after gathering essential information a principal has the necessary prerequisite for deciding what, if anything, is broken, or, better still, what will be broken soon if nothing is done about it. Principals face a continual flow of problems during the course of a school year. Some are short-term and easy to solve, others are complex and require a lot of time and patience. All complex problems require analysis if they are to be solved. In the next chapter we will speak about fixing what is broken—by that we mean analyzing complex problems so they can be effectively solved. We will also discuss creative inquiry—the way to avoid problems before they start.

QUESTIONS FOR REFLECTION

1. John I. Goodlad offers us a list of what he calls the "commonplaces of schooling." After reading the 15 over carefully, see if you can omit one because it has no bearing on your school. Is it true that you can't alter one without affecting the others? Is that Systems Thinking?

2. All principals need data on all the 15 commonplaces but a constant sounding should be taken of the level of satisfaction exhibited by all the stakeholders. Do you think the composite satisfaction rating of school stakeholders is a significant indication of a school's quality? How so?

3. What was Hugh Troy trying to prove? Was he successful in proving his point? What resulted?

4. "The whole process of school renewal rests on the ability of the principal to find out what the administrators, teachers, students, parents, staff, and others impacted by the school know, think, and feel about the institution as it presently exists." How can a principal learn to be a successful prober?

5. How should a principal go about selecting the appropriate sources of information ?

6. Having collected the information, what are some of the best ways of analyzing it ?

7. With greater emphasis placed on site management, explain why the principal and other stakeholders must be more adept at collecting and using information about their particular schools.

8. How does Goodlad's use of his 15 commonplaces of schooling offer a practical way to summarize data? How would
   you apply them to your school?

4

PRINCIPAL AS PROBLEM SOLVER OR, BETTER, PROBLEM AVOIDER

Most of the mistakes of our life come from feeling when we ought to think and thinking when we ought to feel.

We devoted the last chapter to discussing the collection of information. In a sense, this chapter should precede Chapter 3. If the principal hadn't recognized a problem, he or she wouldn't have gone to the trouble of collecting all that information. We collect information in order to solve problems. Right? Well, yes and no. We can say we are collecting information to solve known problems, but we are also constantly collecting data as a feedback mechanism to avoid the occurrence of problems. In this chapter, I will highlight some of the material on Problem Analysis which the National Policy Board published in *Principals For Our Changing Schools.* I would like to go beyond that practical presentation, and spend some time with you on the four ways that principals think. I would also like to point out some ways that principals can improve their skills in creative inquiry.

WHAT IS PROBLEM ANALYSIS?

In the book, *Principals For Our Changing Schools*, Scott Thomson and his team of researchers, headed by James Sweeney, give this definition of Problem Analysis.

> "Problem Analysis: Identifying the important elements of a problem situation by analyzing relevant information; framing problems; identifying possible causes; seeking additional needed information; framing and reframing possible solutions; exhibiting conceptual flexibility; assisting others to form reasoned opinions about problems and issues." (8)

The definition, as stated, should offer any principal a good outline for approaching the analysis of a problem. Remember it is better to solve problems than crises. The steps are logical, reflecting the way our minds are wired. By definition, to analyze means to separate or break up any whole into its parts so as to find out their nature, proportion, function, relationship, etc. The principal studies this information and then frames the problem so it has a beginning, a middle, and an end. One of the smartest thing to do when analyzing a problem is to walk around it so you can appreciate its size. How big is the problem? Newly appointed principals have a tendency to exaggerate the extent of some problems. They often see problems as longer, wider, higher, and deeper than they really are. Walking around a problem helps us realize that though it is big, it is not the end of the world. On the other hand, experience will teach us not to underestimate the size of the problem. Someone once said, "If, in the midst of handling a critical problem, when all around you are losing their heads, you keep calm and collected, it could be that you don't really know how big the problem is or what is really happening."

We know that principals face a continual flow of problems during the course of a school year, month, week, day, and hour. Some are short-term problems which are relatively easy to solve. In fact, with experience many of the lesser problems are handled instinctively by the principal. He or she doesn't even think much about them. Today's small routine problems bear a great resemblance to yesterday's small routine problems. We won't have much to say about these routine problems. Here is where experience pays off. We are more interested in the problems that demand a good deal of careful pondering and the recollection of pertinent facts.

Principals skilled in problem analysis are usually effective problem solvers. They ask the right questions, define and analyze the problem at hand, and increase their chances of success.

To understand what Problem Analysis means, it will help to define both Problem and Analysis. A problem is that which exists in any circumstance in which an individual in charge lacks an immediate response sufficient to meet the demands of the situation. In an organizational problem, we always have a situation which significantly deviates from a goal, plan, standard, policy, or condition which the organization predetermined to be desirable. For example, we have over 20% dropouts. A short definition of a problem goes this way: the recognition of a difficulty or disharmony—the lawn mower dies while you have half a lawn to cut. You have a problem.

Another short definition goes this way: a problem is the difference between expected and actual outcomes. You are making a cake for your son's birthday and you want to surprise your spouse as well. The recipe calls for three teaspoons of double-acting baking powder, by mistake you put in three tablespoons and the cake rises so much it forces its way out of the oven onto the kitchen floor. You have a problem. A problem is something that is unexpected and comes out in a way that contradicts what you wished would happen. As principals you don't need any more definitions of problems. I have never met a principal who didn't recognize a problem when one was staring him or her in the face. "Lights out" principals who misperceive problems need strong assistant principals if they are to survive. Most principals know when a problem is staring at them.

Webster's Dictionary defines analysis as a consideration of all factors; a separation or breaking up into parts; an examination of the parts to find their nature, proportion, relationships, functions, or causes. So Problem Analysis would be the act of becoming aware of an unsettled question or undesirable situation, breaking it into parts, and examining those parts before proceeding to solve the problem. Or, to put it simply, Problem Analysis is the ability to seek out relevant data and analyze complex information to determine the important elements of a problem situation; searching for information with a purpose.

FOUR KINDS OF THINKING PRINCIPALS DO

Now we will step back from the fine lines and paint some broad brush strokes showing how principals think. We will be talking about Problem Analysis but not as the main feature. Although a good principal has to solve problems after analyzing them, principals who will run our changing schools will need to learn to live with Mystery as well as solve problems. Principals who see the world as a series of problems to be solved are often rather dull company.

STREAM OF CONSCIOUSNESS THINKING

Unfortunately, we don't do as much thinking about thinking as we really should. When we do think about thinking itself, the first thing we notice is that our thought moves with such incredible speed that it is almost impossible to push the "Pause" button in order to stop the rapid thought process long enough to have a look at any particular thought or idea. When someone says, "A penny for your thoughts," we usually find our minds are so flooded, it would be difficult, or in some cases embarrassing, to share one thought even if we could capture it. We do a lot of spontaneous thinking or ruminating. Much of our thinking is far too intimate, personal, trivial, or even embarrassing to share. Often, our uncontrolled thoughts concern the self. They are shamefully narcissistic. We see ourselves as being victimized by some unjust power or aggressor, then quick as a wink, we are in charge of the situation and we have rectified the injustice.

As far as we can judge, it seems to most of us that we are thinking all the time during our waking hours, and most of us are aware that we go on thinking while we are asleep. This sleep thinking or self-talking is really dreaming, and it is even more symbolic and illogical than our wakeful daydreams. When uninterrupted by some practical issue, we are usually engaged in what is now known as reverie. This is our spontaneous and favorite kind of thinking. We let our ideas flow freely without constraint. What drives the thoughts in one direction rather than another is usually determined by our hopes and fears, our spontaneous desires, their fulfillment or frustration; by our likes and dislikes, our loves, hates, and resentments. All thought that is not consciously directed otherwise will inevitably circle around our beloved Ego. Because it is so silly and narcissistic we learn to look the other way and miss this reverie of ours. Once you really reflect on it, you begin to realize how much of your time is devoted to it.

Once we get over our shame for having such silly grandiose ideas in our Stream of Consciousness, we start to appreciate what a potent, and in many cases an omnipotent, rival it is to every other kind of thinking. It influences all our speculations in its bull headed tendency to self-magnification and self-justification. Freud taught us that we can gain many worthwhile insights about our character if we learn to analyze our Stream of Consciousness thinking. It is true.

TIRE-PATCHING

Once we go to school we are often roused from this reverie by the teacher who directs our attention to some goal directed task. "Johnny go to the board and print your name in large letters." Parents do the same. Just when you were enjoying a daydream, your mother reminded you to wash you hands and prepare for dinner. With maturity we are faced more often with the necessity of this second kind of thinking. We have to make practical decisions. I have to patch a tire or the car won't go. Shall I fax a document or talk on the phone? Shall we go to Taco Bell or McDonalds for lunch? Decisions, unlike reverie, force us to focus our attention and direct our conscious awareness in one direction. The decision can be a very simple one. In that case we solve it almost instinctively. A principal has been asked the same question or permission so many times, he or she can decide on the answer without leaving the stream of consciousness for long. It is like "call waiting"—quickly we pick up the thread of our reverie. That may work for easy routine problems but not for all problems.

Sometimes problems call for decisions which demand a great amount of careful pondering and the collection or recollection of pertinent facts. This is much harder work than our thinking in reverie, and we sometimes resent this intrusion on our stream of consciousness. We don't like to have to make up our minds when we are tired or absorbed in a happy reverie. Incidentally, weighing a problem in order to make a decision doesn't necessarily add anything automatically to our knowledge-base, although we may have to collect or recollect information before making it. This explains why some people who have worked at a job for 20 years haven't learned much because they have 1 year of experience repeated 19 times. In this chapter we devote some time to such difficult problems and decisions, and move on to even higher levels of thinking.

POLEMIC THINKING

A third kind of thinking is stimulated when any one questions our beliefs and opinions. In areas that have little meaning or value to us, we find it easy to change our minds and go along with others doing something different from what we had planned. We had been thinking of going to McDonalds but someone in the office said, "How about Taco Bell for a change?" We hear the request and rather easily adapt, and go along with the crowd for tacos. It doesn't matter that much to us. When someone challenges one of our deep beliefs or opinions, the situation changes when we are told we are wrong. We resent it, and harden our hearts. We think Polemically.

There is a strange quirk in human nature which inclines us to get our backs up when someone contradicts one of our opinions even if we came by that opinion in the most cavalier fashion. It isn't the idea that is so dear to us, but our self-esteem which appears to be threatened. We will defend this flimsy opinion to the death. We become a disputant.

Few of us take the pains to study the origin of our beloved opinions; rather we have a natural reluctance to check on the reasons we would offer to substantiate this or that opinion. It is like inertia. *We like to continue to believe what we have been accustomed to accept as true.* I can think of no better example than Robert Frost's great poem, "Mending Wall." The two farmers are repairing a stone wall that separates their farms. One of the farmers knows the other to be a stubborn conservative, so he pulls his leg by suggesting perhaps they don't need a fence at all since, as he says, "my apple trees will never get across and eat the cones under his pines." But the old fellow will have none of it, he just repeats over and over again, "Good fences make good neighbors." He probably heard that statement from his daddy when he was young and it has become one of his cherished beliefs. We all do this. When our opinion is contradicted we search frantically for every excuse to cling to it. "Good fences make good neighbors." The result is that much of our so-called reasoning consists in thinking Polemically, finding arguments for continuing to believe what we have always believed. In this way there is no movement in the discourse, and we fail to expand our knowledge and understanding. The Year-Round School won't work. Block scheduling will ruin education. Team teaching is a fad that will pass away. Let sleeping dogs lie. Don't fix what isn't broken. Don't rock the boat.

The real reasons for our beliefs are often concealed from ourselves and others. As we grow we simply adopt unquestioningly the opinions presented to us. We drink them in from our environment and culture. Finding good reasons to justify our routine beliefs is known, since Freud, by the name "rationalizing." This Polemic approach interferes with the next kind of thinking. In order to become a Creative Thinker we have to put aside the Polemic and open our minds.

CREATIVE OR GENERATIVE THINKING

Merely the fact that an idea or opinion is old and has been widely held is an argument in its favor, but this doesn't excuse us from inquiry—making an effort to expand our knowledge and understanding. We must always check to see if we are merely rationalizing. We should be able to have opinions that are the result of honest reasoning out in front of us and allow others to agree or disagree giving their reasons. Sometimes we will be confirmed in our old opinions, sometimes we will examine the reasons and conclude that our opinion isn't worth a hill of beans. Then we should be able to change our minds and look for a better approximation of the truth. These are the steps in knowledge and understanding. They point the way to wisdom.

This leads us to another kind of thinking which can be distinguished easily from the other three. Unlike Stream of Consciousness it doesn't hover about our personal complacencies and humiliations. It doesn't consist of our daily problems which bring with them the demand for Tire-Patching. Nor does it consist in a Polemic defense of our cherished beliefs and prejudices. On the contrary, it is the best kind of thinking because it can lead us to changing our mind and to generative or creative learning.

Creative thinking can raise us to the highest level of human living. On our capacity to expand this kind of thinking depends the future of our race. If we don't learn to use Creative Thinking better, we won't be able to grope our way out of the mess in which most of this earth's civilized people find themselves. In the past, this fourth kind of thinking was called Reason. Unfortunately, since the Age of Reason and the Enlightenment, the word has been so misused we are forced to find a different name. Creative Thinking appears to be a better way to characterize this fourth kind of thinking. This kind of thinking uses meditating and reflecting to yield knowledge, making ideas look different than before. This kind of thinking makes renewal possible. It would be impossible to exaggerate its importance to principals, teachers, and parents. Our mission in the school is clear. Whatever else schools do, they should have as their prime responsibility the task of helping students learn to think creatively, to use reason and feeling well.

There are times when we find ourselves in a "creative thinking mode." It means that we are engaged in observing things or making reflections with almost total disregard for our personal preoccupations. We are not immersed in our own narrow narcissistic world. We are not defending or advocating for some opinion we hold dear. Nor are we apologizing for one of our beliefs. We are just wondering and looking and perhaps seeing what we never saw before. We are creators, discoverers, inventors, seekers after truth; pilgrims in a strange land, we are using our highest human powers. We are most alive and most human. We are most uniquely ourselves.

Excuse the exuberance but that is exactly what principals feel when they are thinking creatively about their school and leading it into new experiences. They sense that the stakeholders are also absorbed in some sweeping vision that energizes them. Everyone seems to have more pep. There is an excitement as the team starts to accomplish things they never dreamed were possible. This excitement is catching. The teachers, parents and students come alive in their Shared Vision.

One of the strongest urges shared by humans is curiosity. We are by nature and by training curious or at least we should be. Most of us were very curious from the time we were born. Watch a baby interact with his or her environment. Babies and young children are like little vacuum cleaners trying to suck up every bit of information they can gather. They are hungry to know. We all have some personal interest in other people's affairs. We are always trying to find a better way to do things. We never leave well enough alone. We can't just let the thunderstorm bring its thunder and lightning. We have to mess with it. In 1752, Benjamin Franklin walked out into a thunderstorm, flew a kite with a key attached and collected an electric charge into a primitive battery. Then, in 1831, an English physicist, Michael Faraday, invented a generator that converted mechanical to electrical energy. Forty-eight years later, in 1879, one of my favorite people, Thomas Alva Edison, succeeded in lighting an incandescent bulb. I have always admired Edison because he was so modest. He said, "I never did anything worth doing by accident; nor did any of my inventions come by accident; they came by work." Edison worked for years and tried every conceivable substance for his filament until he was successful. He had a burning curiosity. But Edison's best quote is: "There is no expedient to which a man will not go to avoid the real labor of thinking."

Seven years after Edison invented the incandescent light bulb, George Westinghouse and William Stanley, in 1886, introduced alternating current (AC) power in Great Barrington, Massachusetts. It was a big improvement over direct current (DC). This led, in 1890, to the newly invented electric chair which was used to execute convicted murderers in the state prison at Auburn, New York. I sat in that very same electric

chair in 1930, when I was 10 years old. In 1935, electricity was
used in the first electric guitar and organ. What will they think
of next? In 1951, we had the first nuclear reactor which could
produce electricity. Human curiosity led to all these inventions.
Some of the results were a boon to our civilization and culture.
Some are more questionable.

A PROCESS MODEL OF EFFECTIVE
PROBLEM ANALYSIS

In the book, *Principals for Our Changing Schools*, the authors
offer a Process Model Of Effective Problem Analysis which will
be helpful for all principals (9). I will summarize this excellent
model with the hope that it will whet your appetite for the real
thing. The *first* thing to note in handling any complex problem
that can't be solved intuitively, is that the outcomes are affected
by *internal and external factors*. External factors include the
availability of information, the urgency to find a solution, the
nature of the organization, the barriers that interfere with
effective problem analysis and the importance of the problem
itself.

Suppose we take an actual problem and apply these steps
to it. In the Rowan-Salisbury School District in North Carolina,
the superintendent, Dr. Donald Martin, was faced with a
problem most superintendents have faced or will face. Many
educators now believe that tracking is not the best way to go
about educating students in K-12. Unfortunately, for 20 years
educators told school systems—and they in turn told parents—
that the tracking of students on the basis of ability grouping
would bring about the best results for all students. Now, how
do we get rid of such tracking without raising the ire of the
parents whose children are among the higher achievers in the
Gifted and Talented groups? These students have had the best
teachers and, in many cases, the best text books, classrooms,
etc. It is a serious problem.

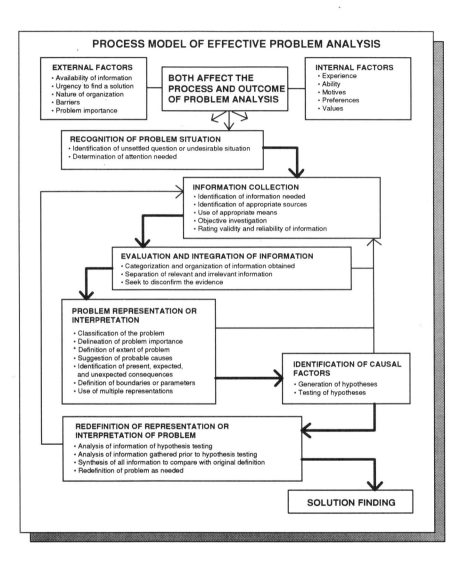

PROCESS MODEL OF EFFECTIVE PROBLEM ANALYSIS

EXTERNAL FACTORS
• Availability of information
• Urgency to find a solution
• Nature of organization
• Barriers
• Problem importance

BOTH AFFECT THE PROCESS AND OUTCOME OF PROBLEM ANALYSIS

INTERNAL FACTORS
• Experience
• Ability
• Motives
• Preferences
• Values

RECOGNITION OF PROBLEM SITUATION
• Identification of unsettled question or undesirable situation
• Determination of attention needed

INFORMATION COLLECTION
• Identification of information needed
• Identification of appropriate sources
• Use of appropriate means
• Objective investigation
• Rating validity and reliability of information

EVALUATION AND INTEGRATION OF INFORMATION
• Categorization and organization of information obtained
• Separation of relevant and irrelevant information
• Seek to disconfirm the evidence

PROBLEM REPRESENTATION OR INTERPRETATION
• Classification of the problem
• Delineation of problem importance
* Definition of extent of problem
• Suggestion of probable causes
• Identification of present, expected, and unexpected consequences
• Definition of boundaries or parameters
• Use of multiple representations

IDENTIFICATION OF CAUSAL FACTORS
• Generation of hypotheses
• Testing of hypotheses

REDEFINITION OF REPRESENTATION OR INTERPRETATION OF PROBLEM
• Analysis of information of hypothesis testing
• Analysis of information gathered prior to hypothesis testing
• Synthesis of all information to compare with original definition
• Redefinition of problem as needed

SOLUTION FINDING

External factors must be faced. The Rowan-Salisbury School System does not have available information which can prove that getting rid of tracking will do no harm to students and can, in fact, help. Believe me this is an urgent problem which cries out for a solution. Most of the collection of information is done at the Central Office level. Individual schools don't have the resources to do large statistical studies. In this case it was fitting that Central Office took the lead.

The Rowan-Salisbury School System researchers were able to demonstrate that local high achievers removed from tracked classes and placed in mixed or heterogeneous groups suffered no academic damage. On the other hand, those students judged to be below average achievers actually profited from being in the same classroom with the high achievers. It appears from this study that if we offer a generous quality education to students, it is better to do so in mixed classes which reflect the world at large. The gifted don't lose (they may even gain in social sensitivity which we don't measure) and the less gifted profit from being in the mainstream. This school system deserves credit for facing an external factor—the lack of availability of information—and solving it with an excellent study. (Not all researchers will agree with their findings.)

One more external factor before we move on. In the town next to the city in which I live, we just had an election for a county school board seat. Only 13% of the voters thought it was important enough to vote. This apathy is an important external factor in school problems. For principals I have one word of advice. You can't educate students alone. Unless, as Goodlad says, we can get a broader based public caring about the public schools we will not be able to fulfill our mission. Later I want to offer you some encouragement about going out into the cities and towns and making a case for public education. Around my territory it is the tax-cutters who are mounting the best campaigns to get elected to the school boards. The future of this country really depends on the quality of our public education. Public support is crucial at this time, and the public hasn't the vaguest idea of what schools are doing today. They need to see and hear from dedicated educators like yourselves.

Internal factors must also be faced. The superintendent of Rowan-Salisbury School System had to determine if he had at

Central Office a person experienced enough in doing this type of statistical study. He did, and he delegated this task to him. He also found he had principals and teachers in the schools who would cooperate in making the study. The team he put together had the ability, the motivation, and the shared values necessary to accomplish the task. They were stakeholders who saw the problem, and knew that a collection of pertinent information was the first step in handling it.

Recognition of the problem is the necessary prerequisite. The research team states the problem well.

> "It is inarguable that educational change is sweeping the nation, including the state of North Carolina, at a breakneck pace. Improved schooling is deemed critical for the nation to survive in an ever increasing globalized economy in which Asian and European competitors are found to produce a better educated student and hence, a more competent workforce. Many individuals have argued that improved tracking systems are the factor that has propelled Asian and European nations to the forefront concerning student achievement. Japan is frequently cited as a 'best practices' example for business, industry, and education; however, it is a fact that there exists no attempt in Japanese schools to track students prior to the tenth grade. Typically, the Asian and European students outperform their American counterparts, not as a result of the enhanced tracking fallacy, but due to longer school days, higher parental expectations for all students regardless of ability, and an over all lengthier school year."

(This quote is taken from page 3 of *The Effects of Untracking the Social Studies Curriculum in Rowan-Salisbury Secondary Schools*— 314 North Ellis St. Salisbury, NC 28144)

Information Collection was well-done by the research team in Rowan-Salisbury. They identified the information needed. They decided on the appropriate sources—their own secondary schools. They used the appropriate means to collect the data. They carried on an objective investigation making certain that it could be replicated. The authors tell us, on page 5, "Results are presented in as unbiased fashion as is humanly possible and with the statistical rigor to back subsequent conclusions." Throughout the study they made explicit the validity and reliability of information.

Evaluation and Integration of Information was carried out in a very professional manner. The authors explained how they categorized and organized the information. They made it clear how they separated the relevant from the irrelevant data. Finally, they fully explained the methods used in the study in such a way that critics could evaluate and agree or disagree with their methodology.

Problem presentation in this study is much more formal and professional than we find in similar studies. Usually, a principal and other stakeholders can grapple with a problem, collect the pertinent information, and make a good decision in a much less elaborate manner. The problem is defined in a clear and distinct manner. Suggestions of probable causes of the problem are advanced with care and moderation. The research team made it clear that the results could have serious practical consequences, and they have. They used the newest and best graphics to make the findings understandable and interesting to the reader.

Identification of Causal Factors was most carefully carried out. Remember, the authors never said that tracking was the single cause of poor achievement in schools. Rather, they were cautious in stating that since Japanese and European schools get good results without tracking, it might be that we in the U.S. could do just as well as we are presently doing without tracking. Then they monitored the untracking experiment. At the conclusion, they declared that test results, comparing tracked and untracked students, seemed to indicate that when a true untracking practice was pursued, the majority of Rowan-Salisbury students responded with improved competencies, most apparent in the areas of Economics, Legal, and Political Systems. They had generated a good hypothesis, tested it, and drew conclusions that seemed to be well-substantiated.

Redefinition of Representation or Interpretation of Problem. In a simpler way, this can be stated as looking back at what was done and seeing where it could have been done better. At the end, the author makes one point clear. Merely untracking without improved instruction will not accomplish the goal of quality education.

When a principal and other stakeholders use this Process Model of Effective Analysis, they must analyze all the information gathered before hypothesis testing and analyze all information revealed during hypothesis testing. This information should be synthesized, and the problem defined, if appropriate. This is stated in a complex way, but it is simply following your natural logic. You suspect that tracking isn't solving any problems and it may well be getting in the way of solving some. So you gather material and make an hypothesis the way the people at Rowan-Salisbury did.

Suppose we have two sections. In one, the groups stay tracked and in the other, the groups are randomly mixed. We then hypothesize that it would not hurt the more gifted students to be mixed and it may help the less gifted ones if they are. Now you have to look at the information collected after a sufficient time has elapsed and see if your hypothesis is confirmed or contradicted. What the principal and other stakeholders do is this: you compare information obtained before hypothesis testing to information revealed during hypothesis testing; encourage others to seek incongruencies in the data; and pose the problem in new terms if the information warrants it. That study by Rowan-Salisbury is a good example, but, as a principal, you don't have to make a study as professional or complete as that one. Your final presentation could be done in three pages with a couple of graphs. What you are trying to do is solve a pressing school problem, and you use logic to do it.

Goodlad firmly believes that the principal and other stakeholders in each school can do the kind of research necessary to give them the internal and external knowledge needed to analyze and solve most problems. Why are the fourth and fifth graders so much less happy in school than they were when they were in second and third grades? First we have to find out if they are less happy. How? Ask them. Second, if they are less happy, what are the causes? What is the school not doing that it used to do; what is the school doing that it didn't used to do? The same question can be asked of the fourth and fifth graders. This type of thinking and problem analyzing should be an ongoing part of the school's educating process.

We do it at home all the time. When one of our own children acts slightly different than usual we are quick to spot it. We probe. How do you feel? Do you have a fever? Come here and let me feel your forehead. Did you eat your lunch ? Are you hungry now? Did something happen at school to upset you? Did you have a fight with Becky? With site management, principals will be called upon to do more of this type of problem analysis. Our model spells out the logical process.

CREATIVE THINKING GIVES THE PRINCIPAL A REAL EDGE

Creativity leaves current knowledge behind and produces something that is new. The new thing doesn't have to be the first of its kind in the world, it can just be new to the principal. Actually, it can be the latter. To the extent that a person makes, invents, or thinks something that is new to him or her, that person may be said to have performed a creative act. I hate to hear a principal say, "I'm not very creative." Everyone can be creative if they stop living inside a little box and begin to see new relationships. Every principal has the potential for creating new ideas, relationships, and objects among the many possibilities of life. When you come up with a better or easier way to do your job as principal you are being creative. You are thinking creatively when you can no longer tolerate an explanation such as, "But that is the way we have always done it in this school."

Suppose you are a principal and you think of "Block Scheduling," and then you apply it in your mind to your particular school. That is a creative act. Suppose you, as a principal, wonder whether it would be a good idea to take the concept of "Global Education" and see if that could serve as an overarching idea for your school. That, again, is being creative.

One of the best ways to improve your creative thinking is to uncover your childhood thinking skills. Of all people, you would think that principals of elementary schools ought to be the most creative thinkers in the country. Afterall, they spend most of their time with youngsters who are expert creative thinkers. Watch an infant girl as she gropes out toward the unknown world. Her mind is open-ended. She doesn't have to put things of the same shape together. If we could recapture the thinking we did when we were young, we would see how much we accepted all things for themselves, regardless of their size, color, or weight. We didn't have to classify things and put them in separate bins. We didn't know that all elephants had to be grey.

Creative thoughts go outside the usual route—put aside the accepted formula, pattern, or recipe. Since children don't have these restrictions they can let their imaginations soar in free flight. As principals getting ready for the 21st century, one of your greatest assets will be the ability to get original ideas from your daydreams. We spend a large amount of our time in a reverie, in which we can often come up with creative ideas that could change our way of looking at the school.

There are a few myths about creativity it might be good to clear up before we end the chapter.

MYTH ONE: ONLY THE BRIGHTEST PEOPLE WITH THE HIGHEST I.Q.s ARE CREATIVE

Original thinking involves nonintellectual factors, such as receptivity to novel ideas, and a knack for making connections that hadn't occurred to someone else. In fact, test results seem to indicate that top scorers on creativity tests average 23 I.Q. points lower than top scorers on intelligence tests. The most creative people often have trouble solving problems that demand sticking to rigid rules to find the answer. It isn't true that those persons with the highest I.Q.s are necessarily the most creative. We could say those with the highest I.Q.s are often less creative than others with lower ones.

MYTH TWO: SOME PEOPLE ARE BORN CREATIVE

They can create easily while others are born uncreative, and will never be able to think creatively. We can all learn to develop the skills of creative thinking and this may well be better than being a good problem solver. Afterall, if we really think creatively, we may prevent many of the problems we are now spending so much time and energy trying to solve. I think the way we are brought up determines how easy or difficult it is for us to be creative. If we were brought up in a perfectionistic family in which everything had to be just so, and we had to follow accepted social practice in all that we thought, said, wrote, or did in later life, we would have to work harder at being creative. Being around young school children can be a great benefit for teachers unless, of course, they feel compelled to tame the children's spontaneity and creativity.

MYTH THREE: ALL CREATIVE PEOPLE ARE LONERS WHO SPEND A LOT OF THEIR TIME DOING NOTHING

Actually creative people do tend to be daydreamers but they are also hard workers. Most of them have a strong nonconformist streak and jealously guard their private moments, but they are not loners. In fact, they seem to need the stimulation of their colleagues and enjoy group discussions which take on the form of "brainstorming." Creative people like to meet with others like themselves.

MYTH FOUR: CREATIVE PEOPLE BLOSSOM OVERNIGHT AND SHOW AT AN EARLY AGE THAT THEY CAN DO CREATIVE THINGS THAT OTHERS CANNOT DO

Although there are some child prodigies, most creative people pay their dues over a long period of time, learning the rudiments of their trade, art, or profession. For example, Leonardo da Vinci spent 12 long years apprenticed in the workshop of Andrea del Verrocchio, a famous painter and sculptor. He spent these dozen years copying the masters and securing the practical education. Like most creative people, it took him many years to become successful. One of the problems today is the failure of many young people to discipline themselves as da Vinci did.

MYTH FIVE: YOU CANNOT RAISE A CHILD TO BE AN INNOVATIVE OR CREATIVE THINKER

The truth of the matter is that you don't have to teach them to be creative. All you have to do is encourage their native creativity. Childhood is the most naturally creative period in anyone's life. When at school we start to teach them the correct solutions and the approved methods, "color inside the lines," then we are putting obstacles in the way of their creativity. How did Verrocchio make sure that Leonardo learned the skills of painting and sculpture without killing in him that creativity which immortalized his works? One of the ways was by exposure to the finest art work available and the efforts to copy it as exactly as possible. Copying would seem to be the biggest obstacle to creativity, but when an artist learns to copy the masters, he or she begins to get the skills necessary for more original and creative work.

Of course we cannot automatically raise a child to be an innovative and creative thinker or doer, but we can enrich and enhance the child's environment with the best examples of music, painting, sculpture, poetry, drama, and stories available; show the child by example how much we relish these beautiful creations; and help the child learn the basic skills necessary to be creative in any of the media which captures his or her fancy. There will be many false starts.

SUMMATION

In this chapter, I tried to offer some aids for problemsolving. The process model, combined with the four kinds of thinking, should prove helpful in solving, and even preventing, problems. In Chapter 5, I will discuss the skill of judgment. The best principals seem to be good at making judgment calls. Their ability to think creatively and analyze problems in a logical way are great helps. As John W. Gardner says, "When top executives are selecting their associates, there are only two qualities for which they should be willing to pay any price: taste and judgment. Almost everything else can be bought by the yard."

QUESTIONS FOR REFLECTION

1. To analyze means to separate or break up any whole into its parts so as to find out their nature, proportion, function, relationships, etc. Good principals have the knack of know-

ing how to assess the importance of different problems. How do they do that?

2. Compare and contrast Stream of Consciousness, Tire-Patching, and Polemic Thinking with Creative Thinking.

3. If a principal allows the trivial to take over center stage in his or her day, there will be no time for the fourth kind of thinking. How can a principal learn to cut down on the first three kinds of thinking and spend more time on the fourth?

4. Rowan-Salisbury School System analyzed a problem and made some policy changes. Was it a good job? Why? Why not? How does it affect your thinking about "tracking"? Not everyone agrees. Why? Why not?

5. Why don't schools in Japan and Europe use tracking? Will they start just as we give up on it? If so, why so? If not, why not?

6. What special training would you need to enable you and your stakeholders to conduct a study like the Rowan-Salisbury in your school? What are your strengths and weaknesses in this area?

7. Am I correct in thinking that many principals have such a narrowly focused idea of research, they believe it can only be carried on by Ph.D.'s or D.Ed.'s with statistical sophistication? Site management demands that the stakeholders in each school do a lot more collection and analysis of pertinent data. Without it they will be driving blindfolded. How can we make this research idea more practical and down to earth?

8. How would you explain to your stakeholders that the five myths concerned with creative thinking are without foundation? What is creative thinking? Why are children so creative?

9. Since all people can improve their ability to be creative, how could you, in particular, be helped to think and act more creatively?

5

THE PRINCIPAL MAKES JUDGMENT CALLS ALL THE TIME

Four dragons guard the cave in which Good Judgment dwells. To gain entrance one must overcome the tendency to submit to faulty and unworthy authority; to be unduly influenced by custom; to succumb to popular prejudice; or to conceal one's ignorance with a showy display of knowledge.

MAKING JUDGMENTS IS WHAT PRINCIPALS DO

Judgment is the key to success or failure for principals. A principal may have many gifts, but if he or she lacks judgment, you can be sure failure will ensue. The major work of a school principal is to make the right judgments at the right time. Incidentally, if it were easy to do this, all principals would be successful. It isn't, and they aren't. Our purpose is to highlight the concept of judgment, show how important it is in the work of a principal, and make some suggestions to help principals measure and improve their skills in judging. We will explain folly and other obstacles to good judgment.

How many judgments would you estimate a busy principal makes in a day? I would not be exaggerating if I said that a principal of a school with 1,000 students and 100 staff members makes 100 significant judgments each day. It could be many more at certain times. Many of these judgments have serious ramifications. They impact strongly on the lives of many people. When Solomon was given a choice as to what gift he wanted, he chose wisdom. There is a close connection between good judgment and the gift of wisdom.

In the world of business, CEOs of large firms are paid handsomely because their judgments determine the profitability of the company. The stockholders judge the CEOs strictly, keeping a close watch on the effects of the CEO's judgments. In schools, a principal's judgments are even more important because they affect the lives of our next generation. It is not easy to measure the quality of a principal's judgments because the results are so complex and intertwined with the input of other agencies—home, neighborhood, media, church, and wider social values. Nevertheless, it is important to improve the judgment skills of principals if we hope to improve schools and help students. Most of the principals I teach are very committed to improving their ability to make good judgments.

In *Principals For Our Changing Schools*, the definition of Judgment is as follows:

Judgment: Reaching logical conclusions and making high quality timely decisions based on the best available information; exhibiting tactical adaptability; giving priority to significant issues.

Most people use the words judgment and decisionmaking interchangeably. They aren't really the same. It is important that we distinguish between judgment and some of its common synonyms. Judgment is not the same as conclusion. True, a conclusion comes at the end of a reasoning process, but judgment includes much more than the conclusion. Also, deduction and induction are only steps in the judgment process, not the process itself. Deduction is a reasoned conclusion based on a given set of principles, facts, or assumptions. The usual distinction between deduction and induction is that deduction is going from universals to particulars and induction is going from particulars to universals. Principals use both inductive and deductive reasoning daily, whether they are conscious of it or not. These are parts of the judgment process, and the better a principal can perform each part, the more successful he or she will be with the whole judgment process.

When I was young we were still somewhat blinded by the flash and glitter of the Age of Reason. We were taught that to make good judgments we had to make sure we excluded emotions, imagination, desires, and all such secondary things. I remember an example which made it clear that reason was king. In judging we were counseled to do what we do when driving a car in the rain. Turn on the windshield wipers—they take away the water so we can see and steer correctly. In making a good judgment, we must clear our minds and hearts of all emotions, desires, hunches, images, symbols, stories, etc., which can only interfere with good judgment. The more we could be objective, the better judgment we would make. I believed that for a long time. In a business school where I taught for 8 years, that theory was pretty much accepted as gospel. Business executives were taught to avoid the "touchy feely" and stick to the objective facts. They were constantly surprised when their judgments were counterproductive. I think most principals realize that it is impossible to be coldly rational in their judgments, yet many feel guilty when they sense that they are making judgments based on hunches, intuitions, and values.

Actually, the classic theory assumes a rationality that just doesn't exist. Rationality is limited by our unconscious skills, habits, reflexes, values, conceptions of purpose, and knowledge. If principals want to make good judgments, they can better spend their time by developing good unconscious skills, habits, reflexes, values, and goals. This insures better judgment than trying to do the impossible—judge as if we were robots. To know yourself better is a step toward judging better.

When principals make judgments they know that better judgments can be made when more information is available, when the principals have more time to weigh criteria, when the dust settles. Most principals like most other executives realize that good judgment is a matter of "satisficing." This is a process for making modestly rational judgments that are not necessarily final. Good principals make better and better approximations. Each judgment is the best they can make at the time. They always keep an open mind, trying to find ways to improve on their judgments.

I like the six steps in decisionmaking in *Principals For Our Changing Schools* (10):

Step	Role of Judgment
1. Define the problem	Judge to identify the big problem and avoid focusing on symptoms
2. Criteria identification	Judge what criteria are relevant
3. Criteria weighing	Judge what criteria are most important
4. Generate alternatives	Judge where and how to search for alternatives and for how long
5. Ranking alternatives	Judge the consequences of various choices
6. Implementing decision	Judge who should implement the decision and when and how the decision should be implemented

Our task in this chapter will be to help principals carry out these steps by offering suggestions for improving the judgment skills involved.

If judgment is a function of interactions between the principal and the task, it follows that the better the principal can grasp the task, know him or herself, and handle the available information, the more successful he or she will be at making solid judgments. In order to accomplish this, principals have to improve on their core thinking and readiness skills.

CORE THINKING SKILLS FOR BETTER JUDGMENT

The core thinking skills include focusing, information collection, organizing, analyzing, integrating and evaluating. Many refer to these as higher order thinking skills and they are essential to good judgment. For a fuller explanation of these, I refer you to Chapter 4 of *Principals For Our Changing Schools*. I would like to offer some suggestions to help principals develop these core thinking skills. In this section, I will cover the preparation of our lives for developing the higher order thinking skills; the storing of the images that contribute to higher order thinking and judging; and finally, the elaboration of these images in our minds in order to make good judgments.

When I graduated from high school in the late 1930s, I discovered I had been able to get through secondary school without doing very much serious thinking or reflection on the thinking process itself. Having been accepted, on probation, in a small liberal arts college, I believed I had a good brain, but I really didn't know how to use it very well. As I floundered in the Fall term, my rescue came by way of a then new book by Mortimer Adler, *How to Read a Book*. Now, more than 55 years later, I still teach this great book to the principals.

The section on Analytic Reading is not so much on how to read as it is on how to think correctly. It is a great help for making good judgments. With my classes of principals and assistant principals, I use Adler's six steps in analytic thinking and apply them to two seminar readings: *The Crito*, one of Plato's Dialogues, and *The Prince* by Machiavelli. The principals really get involved in these interchanges in which they discover how the six steps of analytic reading help them engage in conversation with Plato and Machiavelli. Adler teaches them how to respond to the authors by making their own judgments. As the 2-hour period ends, the principals are involved, excited, and make solid judgments on serious ideas. There is no cookbook way to learn how to judge better. By learning to read, listen, and think better, we fill our minds with good ideas, know ourselves better, and judge well.

By a strange quirk of fate Mortimer Adler, who has always been my intellectual hero, came to teach at the Principals' Executive Program at Chapel Hill. I have frequently had the pleasure of talking with him and listening to him present his ideas on Paideia, and especially on the advantages of Seminar Teaching. I know he was pleased that we were using both his books, *How to Read a Book* and *How to Speak How to Listen*. He wasn't at all pleased to find out that I had written and distributed to the principals a short booklet, *How to Read How to Read a Book*. He saw no need for such a crutch. Since Adler doesn't come to our program any more, I can once again use the forbidden booklet. The principals are happy and so am I.

HOW CAN PRINCIPALS PREPARE THEIR LIVES AND MINDS FOR HIGHER ORDER THINKING?

When we are with others we deal with social thoughts. Most principals spend most of their waking hours in the company of others. Their minds are filled with social thoughts. Now there is nothing wrong with social thoughts. They are the glue of our society. But social thoughts are always framed in "got to's." I have got to get the roof fixed. I have got to hire a new secretary before the end of the month. Social thoughts are practical, operational, action oriented. If, as a principal, you really want to prepare your mind for better judging, you definitely need some time alone. I know how naive this must sound to you. Principals would like to have more time to themselves, but they tell me it is almost impossible for a nonprincipal to grasp how completely the job absorbs all their time. Charles Dickens used to walk for hours and hours through the rainy, deserted London streets. This was his solitude. This is how he replenished his mind. He stocked it with images and ideas. He tells us that he could never have written so voluminously if it were not for the long solitary walks.

How can a principal get the solitude every human being needs? I don't know the answer. Only if you really crave solitude will you get it. If you want it enough, solitude will come, and in it you will feel an exhilaration of consciousness. You will meet yourself. Getting to know yourself in solitude is the first step to higher order thinking and clearer judging. Think of some person you really admire. What traits stand out in that man or woman? The persons we admire are at ease with themselves. They seem to have an inner calm—a sureness of self without arrogance. This I guarantee you, such persons find time to be alone daily. With practice they may even enjoy the solitude of waiting for a traffic light to change. They may meditate standing in line to buy a ticket.

Most principals have found that they do not know how to set limits. All the stakeholders in the school feel free to demand time of the principal whenever they have a need for it. Principals who know how to find and use solitude can be available most of the day, but they have periods when they cannot be disturbed under any circumstances. Slowly, the stakeholders begin to respect this need for solitude, and even brag that their principal is a thinker who needs time to be alone. The principal who demands time for solitude will make better judgments, need less time to collect data, and spend less time cleaning up mistakes.

We have been speaking about exterior solitude. This is a necessary prerequisite for good thinking and judging, but interior solitude, the elimination one after another of all the images foreign to our train of thought, is also important. The real goal of solitude is the growing ability to concentrate or focus our attention.

Adolescents spend much time in what appears to us as daydreaming, because of their urgent need to find themselves. They are striving to gain an identity to be able to think and judge for themselves. Even as principals, you are still striving for the solitude needed in order to be yourself and find yourself. A person can be in his or her mid-fifties or sixties and still not have found a "voice" or a distinctive self. He hasn't craved solitude enough.

When you were 15 you fell in love, deeply in love. You could sit or walk alone for hours and think only of your loved one. You were absorbed in thought but it was more than mere abstract ideas. Your emotions, desires, dreams were tightly connected like a train, and they ran around and around the track of your mind. You were in exterior solitude and you had interior solitude-concentration. You were very much in touch with yourself. You were unconscious of extraneous persons, places, and things. Your mother had to call you three times to get your attention so you would set the table for supper. Your siblings laughed at you and called you "space cadet." We have all experienced this phenomenon.

A principal who has learned to crave and get exterior and interior solitude can be absorbed by the vision of a school. Many of the problems inherent in the planning of that school will seem to solve themselves as she is thinking of fulfilling her vision. It is like an adult love affair. Principals who get great things done have discovered ways to buy both exterior and interior solitude, to concentrate, to be absorbed in a vision, to wall out distractions and to fill their minds, hearts, and souls with images of a higher order.

Principals can learn to concentrate better. This will improve their thinking and judging, but it takes solitude as well as patience and practice. Recently, I talked with a retired principal who was bemoaning that he now has the time to concentrate and read the good books he had planned to read, but somehow he seems unable to do it. Whenever he tries to focus his attention, a flock of irrelevant images flood in and make it impossible for him to focus. He confided to me that the solitude scares him. He doesn't know what to do with himself. When he tries to confront the irrelevant images and drive them away, he feels himself getting anxious and tense. On my way out of the house, his wife whispered in my ear, "See if you can get him interested in something so he'll get out of the house. He is driving me crazy, meddling with whatever I do."

Here is a man who didn't learn to fight for solitude when it was hard to get. He allowed the job to run him instead of his running the job. He never learned to be constructively alone, to experience himself while he was still in the work world. He is paying the price now, but he paid it all his worklife as well.

It is the nature of our mind to superimpose sets of images. They swirl around as in a whirlpool. If they have one thing in common, it is that they are narcissistic. They reflect our fears and desires, and usually make us look good, overcoming great odds. We are the heroes of our undirected home movies. The busiest principal engages in these fleeting reveries, and it is with reluctance that the principal turns off the pleasurable mental rompings to face the cold cruel world. The real trick is learning to control the superimposed images voluntarily without having the daily routine problems force us to think practically.

If our retired principal had learned to seek solitude, and do creative thinking, he would have been a much greater leader in the schools, and he would have had a better retirement. Fortunately, it wasn't too late for him. He joined a local book club devoted to reading and discussing the Great Books. He has attended two sessions, and is now making inquiries about a Master's Degree program in Liberal Arts. His wife is delighted, because he now has a purpose, and directs his insatiable curiosity toward matters other than her daily routine.

WHAT OBSTACLES INTERFERE WITH THE PRINCIPAL'S LEARNING TO DO CREATIVE OR GENERATIVE THINKING?

A serious obstacle to the pursuit of the fourth kind of thinking is our negative self-image, what we used to call an inferiority complex. When a principal listens to a fellow principal give a marvelous lecture on School Climate, he says to himself, "I should be able to give a talk like that. She had the audience eating out of her hand. I know what I will do. Tonight I'll get out my books on public speaking and begin to prepare a talk." By 10 o'clock the principal is wrestling with the first paragraph of his talk on Discipline in the Middle School. He is tired. *He doubts that he could deliver his speech as well as his colleague.* He never felt comfortable speaking in public. He remembers that he should get a list of chairpersons for the school picnic in time for the next staff meeting. A hundred excuses flood his mind drowning this venture in public speaking. These self-doubts, negative self-images act as obstacles to creative thinking in all too many principals.

Another obstacle to creative thinking and good judgment might be called *posing or playing a role.* It is impossible to live in society without playing some roles. We talk and act differently to our infant grandson than we do to the 14-year-old neighbor who delivers our daily paper. The posing I am referring to means something deeper. Some principals never seem to be able to be themselves. They always appear to be imitating someone else or projecting a personal image that is not genuine. Nothing interferes more with creative thinking than the inability to be one's self. You know the type of person who can't admit he hasn't read a book which is being discussed. He can't admit there is some small city in Europe that he has not visited. If the person is constantly playing a role, he can't shake it off, even when he tries to meditate or contemplate. The desire to appear instead of really be, corrupts the legitimate operation of the mind. When we are trying to make an impression, we use our mind differently than when we are honestly trying to search out the truth. If all our energy is poured into the stream of consciousness, tire patching, and polemic thinking, there is none left over for creative thinking. The more persons can be themselves, the better equipped they are to pursue creative thinking and make good judgments.

My friend, the retired principal was always playing the role of hale fellow well met. He was jolly, kind, and very social, but he didn't read, think, or have the courage to say "no." He was playing a role, and when he retired there was no more audience to applaud him. He was frightened in an empty theatre. He had not developed the inner resources needed to live and grow. He didn't take time to learn to find himself, be himself, and let his thoughts and actions flow from a unified source.

Principals who have been fortunate enough to work with children—Kindergarten through fourth grade—have noted that the younger children have a few years of direct vision and immediate impressions. They see things as they really are, and become so moved by them that they carry these experiences with them through life. The youngsters seem to apprehend persons and things directly without any intermediary, and their impressions are so accurate and strong they don't need to go back to the original source of the impression. It is captured in them for life. They are like expensive cameras taking beautiful pictures, perfectly framed, with a freshness that will not last. We were all like that at one time. By about 10 years of age, maybe earlier these days, the children become aware of their elders-parents, teachers, and of their peers. They get the message that they should *imitate* the adults and be acceptable to the peers. In a matter of months or weeks, you see a child who was natural, unselfconscious, and spontaneous begin to imitate others. They become like little men and little women who now have a split mind. They may believe in ghosts, but they are shrewd enough to conceal it if it is not the accepted thing. They will hold on to their father's hand as they walk along the street, but if they see a classmate coming they drop the father's hand.

To use creative thinking and to be a good judge, a principal has to maintain a certain amount of independence. Years ago there was a classic experiment which indicated clearly how much persons are influenced by the opinions of others. This is the type of imitative behavior which interferes with creative thinking. Ten college students were gathered in a room by the experimenters. It appeared that all of them were subjects. In reality, nine of the 10 were in cahoots with the experimenters. Tim was the only naive subject. The object of the experiment was to judge which of three lines of variable length was most like a standard line; or, to state it more simply to match the length of a standard line with three other lines of variable lengths. The subjects announced their judgments publicly, one at a time. It was rigged so Tim always went last. The nine collaborators all gave a prearranged false answer.

There were 12 trial runs, and on each of them Tim either agreed with the majority with their prearranged false answers or acted independently, coming up with a response that went against the nine. Each time he gave in, it was called a *yield*. Each time he held his own, it was scored as an *independent*. If after the 12 trials Tim had not yielded even once, he got scored as Independent. Zero yielding on 12 trials is characterized by Independence. What percentage of college students in this experiment do you think showed this independence? The answer is 25%. Another 25% went with the majority every time, disregarding their own judgment. How can we help students and principals to really trust their own judgment even when the crowd is going against them? To me this is the core of what a good education should give.

When asked to describe themselves, the Independents see themselves as artistic, emotional, original, while the Yielders see themselves as determined, efficient, kind, obliging, optimistic, and patient. Wouldn't it be great if a student or principal could have all the good qualities of both the Independents and the Yielders. If you take a few moments and reflect on this experiment, you may come up with some original ideas about how we can help principals and students to learn to stick with the truth when they know they are right, to yield and change their minds when that is appropriate, and, finally, the wisdom to know which is which. To do this we need the fourth kind of thinking.

There is another obstacle to critical thinking which we have touched upon but should develop more completely. That is *gregariousness*. Gregariousness is much like imitativeness. Americans have a tendency to gather in groups. Some say it was the experience during the pioneer days of having to forage alone that made social gatherings so desirable to the early settlers. Foreign observers say we are the most gregarious people on the face of the earth. Tocqueville, the French observer of things American, argued that, despite our individualism, it was active civic organizations which were the key to our democracy. And there obviously isn't anything wrong with gregariousness in itself. Afterall, we are political beings. The problem comes when we are so obsessed by being with others that we find solitude oppressive.

> *He who is his own best friend, takes delight in privacy whereas the man of no virtue or ability is his own worst enemy, and is afraid of solitude.*
> *Aristotle*

Howard Gardner, the Harvard psychologist, teaches about our seven intelligences or seven intellectual competencies. The last two he calls the Personal Intelligences. Intrapersonal intelligence is involved chiefly in an individual's examination and knowledge of his own feelings, thoughts, ideas, and visions, while the other, Interpersonal intelligence, looks outward toward the behavior, feelings, and motivations of others. We underemphasize both personal intelligences, but we most neglect intrapersonal intelligence. This is close to creative thinking, and it is impossible to develop unless gregariousness is limited to a point where there is time left for Blessed Solitude.

I alluded earlier to the fact that schooling may do exactly the opposite of what it sets out to do. For the last 70 years, I have been either a student or a teacher. For that reason, I speak not as an outsider, but one very much dedicated to the schooling process. Yet, as I look back, I often wonder if I didn't spend too much time trying to "fit in" and be accepted, and too little time developing my own way of looking at the world. I wonder if I didn't feel inferior when I should have been honing my skills and taking more chances. I know I felt that everything worth writing or saying had been said or written better than I could ever say or write it. For sure, I tried to imitate great people, and found myself playing roles when I should have been writing plays. Maybe gregariousness stole too much of my time. I always wanted to write more than I did, but I couldn't say "no" when someone asked me to teach an extra class, give another lecture, do some crisis counseling. Giving time to the students always had a high priority with me. I don't regret the time I gave, but I have a hunch I could have done all I did and still have had more time to meditate and to write. I wish I had learned earlier about the importance of creative thinking. I guess most of us could admit we often let the trivial have more power than it deserved.

How do we tell the highly educated man or woman from the less educated? It isn't merely by clothes, manners, infor- mation, speech. It is chiefly by capacity for resisting another person's thought and defending his or her own views. That is really what we want the school to do—help the student to learn on his or her own, and be able to form clear judgments on what is right or wrong, good or evil. The students need to be able to articulate their conclusions in a civilized manner, being able to offer persuasive arguments for the positions they hold. They should be able to state their positions in such a way that their adversary can point out the flaws in their thinking. They will be open-minded enough to listen and take the criticisms seriously. If they are really educated, they will not just advocate, they will constantly inquire to see if there might not be a better approximation to the truth than the one they presently have. Can we honestly say that our schooling, as we now practice it, is offering students this kind of quality liberal education?

I think I had a fine liberal arts education but it didn't do that for me. Too much of it consisted in memorizing material that someone else had written in text books. The testing almost always rewarded the quick memory and not the critical judgment. So much of it was passive. The arts and music were seldom integrated into the other subjects. We didn't write enough. We took part in few seminars. Debates were more shows of fancy footwork than efforts to understand the matter more fully and learn the truth.

Now I am trying to sort out what were the good things I got. I want to share these insights with you, so you won't waste as much time as I did with inferiority complexes, posing, imitating, overgregariousness, and following the crowd. The way I figure things at this time can be stated as follows: The more you think, the better adapted you become to thinking, and education is nothing if it is not the methodical creation of the habit of thinking. School should train us mentally with the aim of helping us to keep our minds elastic, stretchable. Our education should be balanced between the practical and the theoretical. It may be that in our country we have opted too heavily for the practical. Our students are conditioned to demand the exact answers to all questions. Is there a right answer for every question, and even if there is, does the teacher have it? Significant questions don't have one clear absolute answer, and most honest teachers admit they don't know the answer. Good principals help students think and judge for themselves.

HELPS FOR THINKING AND JUDGING WELL

Remember, our mind is always active on a constant succession of more or less connected images. The quality of these images measures the quality of our thinking and judging. Every person's mind is a picture gallery. We can't see what others have in their picture galleries, we can only infer this by analyzing their speech and behavior. When my wife and I were climbing down from the Acropolis in Athens last October, she overheard the conversation of two young businessmen. They were speculating about the commercial value of the hill on which the Acropolis is perched, high above the city with a splendid view of the Aegean. One suggested it was worth $100 million. The other agreed. Here we were in the cradle of Democracy, the source of much of Western Culture, at one of the most beautiful and historically significant places in the world, and these two young men were speculating on its commercial value. We couldn't see the pictures in their mental art galleries but we could guess that they were filled with dollar signs and Dow Jones Averages.

We are what we think even more than we are what we eat. Consequently, we have to be more careful of the nutritional value of what we place in our minds. We have to choose wisely what images we will hang in our mental art galleries.

We can't stop thinking and judging anymore than we can stop breathing. The good news is that we can choose what kind of air we breathe, and we can choose, to a large extent, what kinds of thoughts and judgments we will live with. In order to accomplish this, we have to be serious about stocking our minds with images of a higher nature.

It is impossible to spend an hour in a room with a woman or man approaching greatness without being struck by the wonderful thoughts that are being expressed. Each of us at sometime has been fortunate enough to share some time with a great thinker. Mortimer Adler is one of the persons whose brilliantly clear mind never ceases to amaze and exhilarate me. Just to sit and listen to him expound on a subject is an experience never to be forgotten. Think for a minute about some person of distinction in whose company you have been, and reflect on how much you enjoyed listening to that person express his or her ideas. Although you and I may not reach that level of greatness, we can choose whether our minds will be filled with the roughly 100 great ideas highlighted by Adler in his Syntopticon or the trivia which spews out daily from the TV. There is no better way to spend our time than by studying the ideas and lives of great people. This is a shortcut for getting into their picture galleries and seeing what preoccupied them.

Students have an uncanny ability to sense when a teacher or other adult shares ideas that ennoble. We underestimate children when we fail to realize that they can spot the banal quickly and accurately. They are bored easily by gray dishwater-type information but they respond immediately to noble ideas. Children get "turned on" by adults who talk and write about interesting persons and things in an imaginative way. Even as adults, we revel in sparkling conversation about ideas that have real meaning and significance. These ideas are so much more entrancing than the Hollywood Minute or the Dow Jones Report. For many of us they even have the edge over the latest gossip about Michael Jackson, Princess Di, or possible trades in the NFL, NBA, and NHL. We all love the exceptional and find the ordinary, daily information rather banal, but the exceptional need not be the freakish, sensational, or violent; it can consist in the juxtaposition of two major ideas we have never heard connected before.

If a principal can't name some great person who is or recently has been having a great influence on his or her conduct, then that principal is passing the verdict "ordinary" on his or her own thought and existence. Earlier, I used the example of Mortimer Adler, as a great person who influences my life. I could offer many others, like Socrates, Plato, Jesus Christ, Thomas Aquinas, Shakespeare, Cervantes, Dante, Jefferson, and Lincoln, on whom I depend for my ideas and images.

In the field of education I have a whole list of great thinkers I lean on and learn from: Adler, Goodlad, Howard Gardner, Sizer, Glasser, Deming, John W. Gardner, Robert Coles, Gabe Moran, Amitai Etzioni, and a half dozen more. These authors share with me their grand ideas and images, and I am fortunate to be able to use them to stock my personal picture gallery. Since I have this terrific supply of good ideas coming in, I can get rid of the mediocre ideas and images that tend to clutter my mind. This mixture gives me a set of standards of excellence against which to judge my own and others' performances. The success of our thinking and judging really depends on our improving our own store of images and ideas?

However, the ideas and images we receive from great thinkers are only the raw material. What we do with them depends on our using our skills, and practice in focusing, information collection, organ-izing, objectifying, remembering, reflection, creativity, reason-ing, emotional control and ethics. When making judgments, it is important for principals to remember that there is more than one answer to most ethical dilemmas, usually several answers. To choose the best or most appropriate one, principals must determine what values are at stake and then select alternatives that support them. Principals are called upon to incorporate ethical considerations in their judgment processes by continually asking themselves, "Is this the right thing to do?" Ethics provide the moral framework for answering such questions.

Hannah Arendt once said that "the aim of totalitarian education has never been to instill convictions but to destroy the capacity to form any." We can conclude this section in no better way than to say that the aim of democratic or liberal education is the opposite of the totalitarian approach. Our aim is to increase the capacity of principals, teachers, parents, and students to make good judgments, to use the fourth kind of thinking to make decisions, and generate convictions.

THE MARCH OF FOLLY IN THE SCHOOLS

Sometimes it helps to explain a thing by contrasting it with its opposite. When we search for the opposite of good judgment we come up with the idea of folly. One of my favorite writers, Barbara W. Tuchman, wrote a book entitled *The March of Folly*, which delighted millions of readers. I would love to delve deeper into it but in the limited space available I will simply take one of her insights and try to apply it to the field of education.

Barbara Tuchman, the historian, is trying to figure out why intelligent mental processes seem not to function. She wonders why the holders of high office so often act contrary to the way reason points and enlightened self-interest suggests. For instance, why did the Trojan rulers command that the suspicious looking horse be dragged inside the city gates despite every reason to suspect a Greek trick?

Most of us in the field of education would not have to look far to find examples of folly in our field. I gave an example earlier. For the longest time we tried to convince parents, school boards, anyone who would listen, that the best way to teach children is to test them, track them according to intellectual ability, and keep them segregated from peers with less or more measured ability. A better example of folly would be hard to find.

Tuchman gives criteria for deciding whether or not the judgment qualifies as true folly. The policy adopted must meet three criteria: it must have been perceived as counterproductive in its own time, not merely by hindsight. Second, a feasible alternative course of action must have been available. Third, the policy in question should be that of a group, not an individual guru, and it should persist beyond any one political lifetime. See if you can list three follies in public education that fit these three criteria. I gave you one: tracking. How about the following? Should every child start kindergarten on the same August day closest to their fifth birthday? Should report cards with numbered scores be given K through fifth grade? Should children compete with each other, and schools compete with each other, despite serious demographic inequities? Should we mark on the curve? Or are these follies?

Folly is a child of power. Power breeds folly. Sometimes those in power are so blinded by what they want, they fail to listen to advice, lapse into unthinking certitudes, fail to use the fourth kind of thinking, close their minds and become wooden-headed. As a result they commit folly. They spend their time defending their bad decisions and refuse to accept criticism. Having forgotten that the overall responsibility of power is to govern as reasonably as possible, they do what the leaders of Troy did—open the gates to their enemies. School leaders have the duty to use power wisely, and there is no better way of doing it than to use Barbara Tuchman's three guides. Listen to the criticism of those who think your plan is counterproductive. Search for feasible alternatives to your first choice, and, finally, involve all the stakeholders in the decisionmaking.

SUMMATION

In this chapter, I reviewed the core thinking skills for better judgment and the obstacles to creative thinking. As we move on to Chapter 6, it might be good to recall that the principal seldom acts as a solitary agent. We know that with site management, the need to develop broader leadership is greater than ever. Assuming the principal is very skilled in judgment, she or he must also develop the stakeholders so they, too, will have the ability to make good judgments on their own. This can be accomplished best by changing the school into a true Learning Organization. I will explore the Learning Organization in depth with you in Chapter 6. A Learning Organization has many safeguards against folly; more importantly it spends its time creating its future rather than cleaning up its mistakes.

QUESTIONS FOR REFLECTION

1. Why is the ability to make good judgments the key to a principal's success or failure?

2. *Principals For Our Changing Schools* makes it clear that making good judgments requires the ability to reach logical conclusions, to make timely decisions based on the best information, to choose good strategies and tactics, and, finally, to prioritize significant issues. Which of these is the most difficult for you? Why?

3. Why can't principals be coldly rational in making judgments? Why should they spend time developing good, unconscious skills, habits, reflexes, values, and goals?

4. Using the six steps in decisionmaking and the role of judgment involved as an outline, apply them to a serious judgment call you are required to make at the present time. Does this help?

5. Why is a certain minimum amount of solitude necessary if we are to grow in our ability to judge well? How do interior and exterior solitude differ?

6. A principal who has learned to crave and get exterior and interior solitude can be absorbed by his or her vision of a school. Why is it that a compelling vision makes us want to be alone so we can reflect, contemplate, dream, think, and plan?

7. It is the nature of the mind to superimpose sets of images that swirl around as in a whirlpool. How can principals train their minds to the point where they can control the superimposed images voluntarily without waiting for crises to force them to do so?

8. Spending time with great persons and great ideas helps us improve our ability to judge. Why?

9. What are the obstacles to creative thinking? Which two bother you most?

10. Explain why our greater use of Creative Thinking can save
    us from folly?

6

OVERSEEING A LEARNING ORGANIZATION

*You don't learn anything the second
time you are kicked by a mule.*

If some principal had imitated Rip Van Winkle and fallen asleep 20 years ago, what would he or she find upon waking now in the last decade of the 20th century? You remember the story: Rip and his dog, Wolff, wandered into the Catskill mountains before the Revolutionary War. There they met a dwarf, whom Rip helped carry a keg. They joined a group of dwarfs playing nine pins. When Rip drank from the keg, he fell asleep and wakened 20 years later. When he wandered back into town he found his wife had died, his daughter had married, and the portrait of King George was replaced by one of George Washington. He had fallen asleep a subject of the British Crown, and awakened a citizen of a new American republic. It is a great story for illustrating contrasts between older and newer societies. How do principals, who ran schools 20 years ago, see changes today in the way schools are or should be run?

One of the first changes Rip Van Principal would see is that the school board, superintendent, and central office have delegated to the principal much greater power and authority. Principals have a lot more to say about the goals of the school, the allocation of resources, the formulating of procedures and regulations, the empowering of others in the school, and the evaluation of school outcomes.

Why is this so? It is a truism that few people voluntarily yield power and control. Why then have school boards, superintendents, and central office staffs been so generous in sharing power? The answer is simply that the schools were not accomplishing their goals as long as the power was centralized and remote from the school site. Most sensible analysts agree that site management is the only way to go. This doesn't mean we have figured out the best way to do site management. It does mean that the job of a principal has changed drastically in the last 20 years. What would our Rip Van Principal think if he awoke to find that he was now in charge of the school as he had never been? My guess is he would say, "Please, help me retool. We were never trained to do this kind of management or leadership."

A second thing our Rip Van Principal would perceive is that schools are really in a constant transition. When he went to sleep, our principal ran a school that was quite predictable. The planning was done in meetings attended by the School Board, superintendent, and selected members of the central office professionals. The resulting plans were handed down to the principals who were told to implement the plans with the resources that would be allocated to them as well as with plenty of precise procedures and regulations. Empowerment was not a word that was bandied about in those days and the evaluation of school outcomes would be done by members of the central office staff. Test results from Princeton, NJ, the Vatican of public education, would make or break a school and/or principal.

Now the principal awakens to a school in which he is asked to have a vision, develop a Shared Vision, incorporate community values in the individual school plans, empower his associates, and find suitable ways to evaluate the school's achievements. For a principal trained 20 or 30 years ago, change was a dirty word. Change is what got you written up in the local paper. This was not what the School Board wanted. A good principal was dedicated and committed to the status quo. Principals were not trained to be social architects, organizational designers, systems thinkers.

Another change our awakened principal would note would be his or her lack of real power. Although he or she was given complete responsibility, there would still be a 1,000 hidden or semihidden restraints and interferences that would make it more and more impossible to carry out the grand new conception. With a tight economy, teachers' salaries are still low. Physical science teachers are in short supply. The counselors are covering four and five schools instead of one or two. Some parents are banning books. Others are tailoring the curriculum to their peculiar moral needs. Some young teachers are very touchy when corrected. Many students seem to be more hyperactive with shorter attention spans. One in four or five students is poor and hungry. The principal is forced to become an expert in Federal, State, County, and City law. Our Rip Van Principal is strongly tempted to go back to the Catskills and play nine pins with the dwarfs.

Our awakened principal would be fortunate, indeed, if his school system would send him to a four day workshop by Drucker, Senge, Covey, or one of the other organizational gurus who are preaching to the business community. These thinkers are trying to get leaders in both the public and private sectors to wakeup and smell the roses. They are the apostles of Paradigmatic Change. Following the late W. Edwards Deming, they talk about Total Quality and other such topics, but their real message is that the way we have managed organizations in the past is no longer suitable. They agree that managers will become leaders only when they reperceive their world and the relations they have with it. They are telling CEOs to think differently, and learn to see their companies, offices, agencies, and schools as living organisms rather than inanimate machines. Gurus are trying to teach managers to become leaders by using Systems Thinking, and understanding that change is not the exception but the rule.

Schools have changed more than factories or offices, but few principals have been trained in this new philosophy of leadership. It is still possible to run a business using the old pyramidal, mechanistic model with the thinking done exclusively at the top, while the rank and file are programmed like robots. It is absolutely impossible to run a school in that way, and it always was. Our Rip Van Winkle principal who is given a sabbatical to study leadership should rejoice that he or she was coming back to the schools at a time when great results could be accomplished with small leverage. "It is the worst of times, it is the best of times."

With all the difficulties facing them, principals today are in a better position than ever before. They do need much more training and support, but they are leaders in an age in which they can grow and help teachers and students to get ready for the kind of learning that will be demanded in the 21st century. They can truly build learning organizations, which is what schools were always supposed to be.

The definition of Organizational Oversight, offered by David A. Elandson, and his team from Texas, in *Principals For Our Changing Schools,* should be helpful to principals. "Organizational Oversight: Planning and scheduling one's own and others' work so that resources are used appropriately, and short and long-term priorities and goals are met; scheduling flows of activities; establishing procedures to regulate activities; monitoring projects to meet deadlines; empowering the process in appropriate places." (11) They note that poor managers focus on yesterday's problems, good managers focus on today's problems, and truly outstanding managers focus on tomorrow's problems. When you lead a Learning Organization the process itself is directed to recreating, reinventing, and renewing the organization to create a future with no problems at all. Managers think too often of damage control, and fixing what is broken. They ought to focus on building self-renewing organizations in which problems need play no significant part. Do it right the first time is good advice, whether you are talking about workers in a factory producing automobiles or teachers in school trying to produce life-long learners. Deming and the other gurus make it clear that 80% of mistakes are systemic. Poor management creates policy and procedures which in turn cause the errors. Only 20% of miscues are the result of human error or bad will. Deming is very strong in his condemnation of the top management in the American automobile industry. They blamed workers for everything that went wrong, while their own blindness caused them to set up systems that had errors programmed into them.

ORGANIZATIONAL OVERSIGHT

In *Principals for Our Changing Schools,* we find a process model of Organizational Oversight which is helpful (12). Beginning at the top of the model, it proceeds in the following manner. Organizational Oversight, the process that serves it, and the outcomes to be expected from it, are affected by external and internal factors. This fits in neatly with the new biomedical model which is the foundation for much of the newer thinking about management and leadership. In *Webster's Unabridged Dictionary,* an organism is defined as any living thing or anything resembling a living thing in its complexity of structure and function. The school as a living thing is very much dependent on its inner and outer environments. The internal factors include, among others, the ability of a particular school's principal and the school's culture, the stakeholders' experience and ability, strengths and weaknesses.

The external factors include the size and complexity of the school, the resources available to it, and the social pressures that operate on it. How can school systems continue to build schools for over 1,000 students? This is a perfect example for one of Barbara Tuchman's examples of folly. Every shred of evidence points to the fact that small schools run better than large ones. In a class of 40 principals, I ask how many run schools with over 1,000 students? A few raise their hands. Then I ask how many run schools of 800, 600, 400 students. By now all but two have raised their hands. Finally, I ask how many run schools with an enrollment of less than 350? The last two raise their hands and smile. I ask why they are smiling. They answer in unison, "I feel like I died and went to heaven. Small schools are just so much more enjoyable and friendly." Principals believe from experience that you can do much more for students, parents, and teachers if you have a small school. I realize that there may be financial reasons for building larger schools, but is it cost effective in the long run? We now realize that the small, one room school house had much to recommend it.

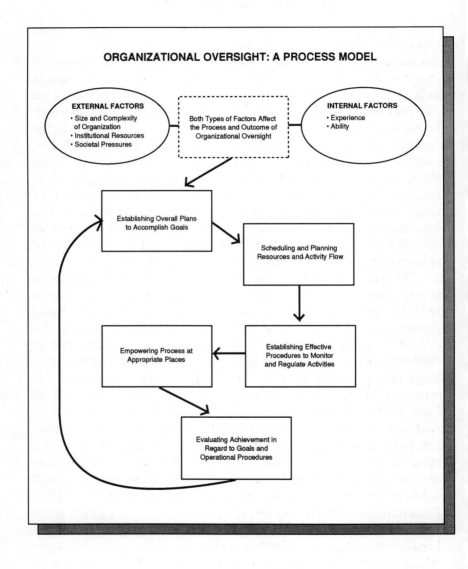

ORGANIZATIONAL OVERSIGHT: A PROCESS MODEL

EXTERNAL FACTORS
• Size and Complexity
  of Organization
• Institutional Resources
• Societal Pressures

Both Types of Factors Affect
the Process and Outcome of
Organizational Oversight

INTERNAL FACTORS
• Experience
• Ability

Establishing Overall Plans
to Accomplish Goals

Scheduling and Planning
Resources and Activity Flow

Empowering Process at
Appropriate Places

Establishing Effective
Procedures to Monitor
and Regulate Activities

Evaluating Achievement in
Regard to Goals and
Operational Procedures

We know that the external factors, among others, include size and complexity of the organization, institutional resources (it is better to be principal in a school that has air conditioning and teachers who really care), societal pressures (it is so much easier to lead a school in which the students don't bring guns to class). These external factors definitely affect process and outcomes of organizational oversight.

Next in the process model on Organizational Oversight we come to strategic plans that are goal-oriented. Before principals can do strategic planning, they must create and share a vision of what the school should be in the ideal order. With a Shared Vision in place the stakeholders must establish overall plans to accomplish goals. Then they schedule planning resources and activity flow. This establishes effective procedures which empower the process at appropriate places. Finally, oversight is completed by evaluating achievement in regard to goals and operational procedures. It isn't simple, but it is logical. Later in this chapter we will discuss mental models and values which are becoming important means for understanding the way team members in a learning organization implement the vision and attain the goals.

Our Rip Van Principal would be amazed to hear how often the word empowerment is used in speaking about leadership in a learning organization. The authors speak about empowering process at appropriate places. I will devote some time later in the book to team building—the best means of empowering the process.

Following Deming, we claim it is folly to depend too heavily on inspection in order to achieve quality. He advises us to build quality into the product or service in the first place, thus eliminating the need for mass inspection. There will always be a need to get feedback, but it is better to get it during the process instead of waiting until the end of the marking period to find out how things have gone. I will introduce some of Deming's other ideas later in this chapter. One of his main ideas is to drive out fear.

How Principals Create Learning Organizations

We ask again what would our Rip Van Principal want? He or she would want some help in retooling. Principals want to study the 21 domains of knowledge and skills recommended in *Principals For Our Changing Schools*. Today's principals are quite aware that they are being asked to do some difficult things: create a vision, share that vision which should incorporate local community values, empower associates, involve parents and the broader community, find ways to continually fund innovations, discover suitable ways to continually evaluate all aspects of the school's programs, train staff in team work, guide the school into a niche in which it can do the most for students while recognizing the limitations within which it must work. I think the modern principal is being asked to create a new type of school. I follow Peter M. Senge, the Director of the Systems Thinking and Organizational Learning Program at MIT's Sloan School of Management, in calling the new type of school a Learning Organization. In his *Fifth Discipline*, Senge offers us the clearest definition of a Learning Organization and outlines the means of creating one. We will discuss some of his ideas on transformative leadership in Chapter 7.

The first mark of a Learning Organization is that all the stakeholders are learners. For me, the basic meaning of a Learning Organization can only be understood if we rethink what "learning" itself means. Learning entails a metanoia or a deep changing of the mind. When we grasp the deeper meaning of the word "learning," it becomes clear that it involves a lot more than merely taking in information.

Adler explains that the goods of the mind are information, knowledge, understanding, and wisdom. The more we acquire these goods the better we perfect our minds. We know that these four are not of equal value. Rather, just as named, they ascend in a scale of values. Information has the least value, wisdom has the most. If we want to build a Learning Organization, we must use all four "goods of the mind," but we will wisely spend more time and energy on knowledge and understanding, and less on information. This is not the case in many American schools.

Unfortunately, as a result of our modern glut of information we somehow mistake information processing for real learning. The awakened principal realizes that he or she must learn how to do some things. If they merely read a book about oil painting, they certainly wouldn't claim that such reading would make them oil painters. Information and knowledge are prerequisites, but the real metanoias wait on understanding and wisdom with praxis. As the awakened principal goes through a series of real learning experiences, he or she will be a new person thinking and acting differently.

The awakened principals, who are learning as never before, will have visions for their schools which they will share with a community of learner-stakeholders, who themselves are also going through series of mind changes or learning experiences. In a middle school with 1,000 students and 100 adult associates, all 1,100 stakeholders will be engaged in the active pursuit of learning every day. Much time will be spent on assimilating knowledge and working toward deeper understanding. The wisdom comes later. Every person in a school must be an active learner if we are to have a true Learning Organization.

Sometimes the school maintenance personnel model the need for continual learning better than some of the academic teachers. In maintenance, the technical changes demand new learning, so the maintenance crew goes to training sessions. Their knowledge-base widens. They begin to understand new principles and procedures, and they experience many metanoias. Meanwhile, back in the classroom, the English teacher continues to let his fingers do the walking through the yellow pages he copied in graduate school 20 years before. In such cases, students aren't motivated and, consequently, there is no real learning, no metanoias, no deepening of understanding, and no appreciation of the material covered.

All four modes of knowing are alive and well in the Learning Organization. Every stakeholder is personally committed to accessing information, to acquiring knowledge, supplementing it with understanding, and attaining wisdom. These are acts of intellect and reason. Acquiring information is only a function of memory. We certainly pay tribute to memory. We can't learn much without a well-functioning memory, but the real work of a Learning Organization is involved with knowledge, understanding, and wisdom.

THE ROLE OF VISION IN A LEARNING ORGANIZATION

The first step the awakened principal takes in fashioning a school into a Learning Organization is an act of the imagination. We know from experience that principals can't change schools singlehandedly. In order to develop any organization, it is necessary to get the stakeholders involved in the project. In order to build a team, the principal needs to have a vision of what he or she would like to have the school become. So the principal starts off by imagining the possible. What would this school be like if it used all its potential to help the students become life-long lovers of learning. The world runs on visions. If a principal lacks a vision for his or her school, someone else's vision will carry the day. Teams function well together only when they are committed to a Shared Vision. Each team member having a personal vision, finds that the principal's vision of the school overlaps significantly with his or her personal vision. There is a match. In fact, the shared vision helps the teacher to stretch his or her vision to meet the wider school vision now beginning to be shared by all the stakeholders. There is a creative energy which bubbles up in such an organization. Experiencing it renews your faith in human nature. People do want to work hard to accomplish something lasting. They will make sacrifices, submerge their own egos, reach out to help others in ways that they never thought were possible.

How can we help principals to use their imagination to create a vision which will inspire the other members of the Learning Organization? It doesn't mean that the principal alone exercises imagination, all the stakeholders should contribute to the shared vision through discussion.

People often have great difficulty talking about their visions, even when the visions are clear. I often wondered why that was so. We are reluctant to talk about our visions partly because we are so acutely aware of the gaps between our visions and reality. It becomes almost embarrassing to talk about the ideal school that we have in our minds and hearts.

Most principals do have a vision or visions of the school they would like to head. The visions aren't original. They are a combination of the best things the principal can imagine happening to a school. These things exist in other schools, but not all together. In the principal's vision, he or she sees improvement in the way the school district is run, the way the classrooms are organized, the use of time, the measures of achievement, the assignment of students and teachers, the way the school relates to its surroundings, and, finally, the way we hold all stakeholders accountable. When the principal sees how far the school is from the vision, there is a tendency to avoid thinking about the vision, much less talking about it. Although the gaps may make a vision seem unrealistic or fanciful, we must confront the gaps or we won't have a vision. These same gaps that can sap our energy when we think of them in the wrong way, can be a source of energy to us when we look at them from the right angle. If there were no gaps, there would be no need for any action to move forward to the vision. People without vision have no creative energy. They are satisfied to let others determine their future and the future of the organizations in which they work. We need to learn how to hold a creative tension in our lives. Great principals do this instinctively. They are perfectly aware of the gaps but they never let go of the vision.

If you imagine a rubber band stretched between your left hand held up palm side down and your right hand held the same way about six inches below the left, you will see that the rubber band is stretched so there exists some tension. Let the left hand stand for your vision of the school as it could be, and your right hand for the present school reality. If you give up on the vision the tension goes out of the rubber band because you lower the left hand. It is easy to relieve the tension simply by giving up on any vision. However, you can also relieve tension simply by raising the level of the right hand—the real school. There are only two possible ways for the tension to resolve itself: pull reality toward the vision or pull the vision toward reality. What happens will depend on whether the principal can hold steady to the vision.

There is no way I can prove this to you, but if you have experienced the exhilaration of being committed to something bigger than yourself, being a contributing member of a team which really cared and was able to accomplish great things through a Shared Vision—a championship season—you will recognize the truth in the above example. When an organization really pulls together for a common cause, the members work harder than usual, but, instead of being fatigued, they become more energized. We talk so much about stress, many people feel that all tension is bad. On the contrary, without a certain amount of tension we lose our muscle tones, we get weak and flabby. It is this creative tension, which arises from the gap between real vision and what is now present reality, that pumps us up and gives us the opportunity to perform above our ordinary level. Vision is a liberator. It frees us from constraints which interfere with our best efforts. If we don't distinguish emotional tension (stress) from creative tension, we have a tendency to lower our vision. Principals realize that when they begin to feel emotional tension (stress), they can always relieve it by adjusting the one pole of the creative tension which is completely under their control at all times—the vision. Their goals are now much closer to current reality. Escaping tension is easy. Unfortunately, the price they pay is to abandon what they really want, their vision.

Most principals that I know are willing to suffer some tension in pursuit of their visions. They tell me that it isn't easy, but it is fulfilling. They are so proud that they were able to hold to a vision that differed greatly from current reality. They opted for the "fundamental solution." They took action to bring reality into line with their vision. They did it by sharing the vision with their team. They are quick to give credit to the work of the stakeholder-team. They caution other principals that changing reality takes time. There is always the temptation to take the "symptomatic solution" of lowering the vision to bring it in line with current reality. They all agree that having a vision of what can and should be is the prime requisite for creating a Learning Organization.

WHICH COMES FIRST? VISION OR VALUES?

Values are attitudes for or against some policies, programs, methods, practices, persons, places, things, events, etc., which have a great influence on what the principals decide to accept or reject in their visions. If a principal or teacher is to change his or her vision, there will have to be value changes as well. A teacher who values silence, order, and control in the classroom may have some difficulty with a principal's vision that includes seminars, cooperative learning, and role playing. Likewise, values play a very large role after the vision is formed and shared. When we have a team of stakeholders agreeing on a shared vision, we can assume that they share many values in common. Now, when the vision is about to be implemented, values again enter the picture. When the team begins to debate on the best way to accomplish the vision, we once again see how important values are. The means to be used will be determined by the goals, objectives, strategies which are chosen. Values shared by the principal and other stakeholders will also determine these choices. We can say that the way a vision is implemented will be a matter of values, just as the vision itself was a product of the values held by the visionmakers. In preparing principals to be change agents and social architects, we would do well to spend more time studying the role of values and visions.

Brendan Gilligan is a principal who says it like it is. Two years ago when I was lecturing on values and trying to explain why values are such an essential part of the principal's vision, Brendan interrupted me to ask a pointed question. "What," he asked, "do you hold to be the highest value in schooling?" To say I was flabbergasted would put it mildly. I fumbled around but failed to come up with an answer satisfying to Brendan or myself. After class I invited him to have a cup of coffee and pursue the question more fully. Brendan, a sincere young principal, was not one satisfied by garden variety educational jargon.

After an hour of spirited conversation we both agreed on our top value in schooling. Realizing that this value couldn't be expressed merely in words, we searched for an image, a picture, a scene to express it. Our top value was simply the relation between the student and the teacher. So we pictured a student and a teacher sitting on a log together. The teacher is showing the student how to do something, while other students were busy working together in teams or just observing nature alone. We agreed that if we could strengthen the relation between the teacher and students, and the relations among the students, and the relation of everyone to nature, the rest of the larger structures would fall into place. When the teacher and students relate well as they learn to do things together, all is well.

VISIONS AND VALUES ARE ESSENTIALLY MENTAL MODELS

When a principal is trying to create a school that will be a true Learning Organization, he or she must take into account that it takes a long time to help people change their minds. Moreover, the principals must realize that obstacles to change exist below the level of consciousness. If principals agree that the prime value involved in changing a school into a Learning Organization is the quality of the relation between the student and teacher, we could call that a value or an ingrained assumption. When Brendan Gilligan, now a nationally known education consultant, goes around the country advising school systems on how to change, part of his baggage is the picture of a student and teacher sitting on a log learning together to do something. He has espoused that value or assumption so long, he seldom thinks about it consciously. He just assumes this to be true. He even assumes that everybody thinks this way.

When he converses with a school superintendent hostile to his ideas, Brendan often wonders why the superintendent opposes what to Brendan seems so clear and obvious. The solution may lie in the Mental Model this superintendent carries in his or her unconscious and also Brendan's Mental Model. Suppose the superintendent's prime value is control. He prefers a classroom with 27 students sitting in rows and the teacher in front exerting vigilant control. To this superintendent, Brendan's image of a teacher and student sitting outside the classroom on a log with no text book, and other students milling about in a disorganized fashion, would be unthinkable. The super-intendent and Brendan disagree because of a clash in Mental Models. Only when Brendan and the superintendent are able to expose their Mental Models, examine them, and change them when appropriate, will they be able to agree on a vision for the school. We change schools only after changing our Mental Models.

With all the talk about values, I was always struck by the implicit assumption that all values are good values. I can think of a lot of values which in my opinion are evil. Here is a sample of what I believe to be bad values.

All children are not educable.

The primary cause of learning is the activity of the teacher.

Didactic teaching of subject matter is the key to good education.

The acquiring of information is the prime goal of schooling.

Competition between students is the best motivator of learning.

A school should supply its graduates with all the learning they will need for a life time.

These values are to my mind bad and dangerous. I hear you saying, "Who in his or her right mind holds these values?" Brendan, who travels nationwide helping schools, tells me that he runs into these mental models all the time. It is true that most people don't come out and make these outlandish statements. The educators who act as if they believed these assumptions may not even be aware they espouse them. It is important for all principals interested in running a Learning Organization to become more familiar with Mental Models. Unexamined Mental Models are a fierce obstacle to forming a Learning Organization.

Mental Models are deeply ingrained beliefs, assumptions, generalizations. They are often expressed in the mind as pictures, scenarios, images. These Mental Models influence how we perceive the world and how we take action in it. More often than not, we are unaware of our Mental Models or the effects they have on our behavior. Racial prejudice is an example of a Mental Model. People of all races entertain Mental Models of their own race as positive and other races as negative. These are not reasoned conclusions, yet they strongly influence the way we perceive and get along with others. Most of the opposition to school renewal can be traced to the Mental Models of stakeholders who have unquestioned assumptions not unlike the ones I listed above.

Schools won't change much until principals can look rigorously at their own Mental Models. At PEP, one of our best components is the opportunity for principals to talk to each other outside of the classroom. It is there that they carry on learningful conversations in which they balance inquiry and advocacy. They expose their own thinking, making it open to the influence of others. Within these conversations, the principals risk surfacing, examining, and changing their Mental Models. It is in these dialogues that deep learning for understanding occurs.

Our mental models determine not only how we make sense of the world, but how we take action. It is now clear that although people don't always behave consistently with their "espoused theories" (what they say they believe), they do behave consistently with their "theories in use," which are their Mental Models. Unless we know our Mental Models we don't know ourselves. It is only by holding up our Mental Models to the mirror and scrutinizing them, that we can begin to know how close or how far our Mental Models are from the truth. That is why dialogue and conversation are so important. Our approximations of the truth can always be improved upon by listening and trying to understand better what others see as true.

Why are mental models so powerful in affecting what we do? The main reason is that they seriously affect what we see. If we have a Mental Model that says all sailors are drunks, we will see any sailor who staggers down the street. On the other hand, we can walk past 100 sober sailors and not see one of them. We see only that which confirms our mental models. Einstein once said, "Our theories determine what we measure." For years, physicists conducted experiments whose results contradicted the teachings of Newton, yet no one "saw" the data produced which eventually led to the triumph of quantum mechanics and relativity over classic physics. Einstein, himself, died unable to reconcile the fact that his theory of relativity took the floor out from under classic physics. Even genius-like Einstein found it hard to sacrifice his Mental Models. What must be true of lesser lights like us! To change Mental Models we need dialogue.

DIALOGUE AND DISCUSSIONS DEVELOP THE TEAM APPROACH

What characterizes the team members in a Learning Organization is their constant commitment to continued learning. For these reasons, it is not a surprise to learn that dialogue and discussion are the two legs on which the Learning Organization stands and walks.

Scientists today will tell you they do their work in teams. Heisenberg, famous for his "Uncertainty Principle," said that science was rooted in conversation. He recalled a lifetime of conversations with Pauli, Einstein, Bohn, and the other great figures who eventually uprooted and reshaped traditional physics. Heisenberg acknowledged that in these heated discussions and dialogues many of the theories that made them famous were conceived. In his old age, he recalled these conversations in vivid detail and with warm emotion. They illustrated for him, and hopefully for us, the awesome potential of collaborative learning. Heisenberg, like many great creative thinkers, acknowledges that the group conversing together can be more insightful and more intelligent than the members could ever be working individually. It is true in a school as well.

The principal and stakeholders work together in teams and use dialogue and discussion, to create "mental maps" for guiding the school. The very learning process that characterizes the principal and stakeholders is modeled for the students. The content of what is learned in school may or may not be serviceable a decade or two later, but the skill of creative and generative learning, grasped through rich discussion and dialogue, will serve them throughout life.

The team members in a Learning Organization learn constantly with and from each other. They are humble enough to realize that, like the blind men describing an elephant, each of them is liable to have only a partial view of the whole. It is only through the continued use of discussion and dialogue that an organization can stay in touch with its changing world, both internal and external.

The principal developing his or her stakeholders to be team members in a Learning Organization needs to understand that there are two primary types of discourse necessary for learning—dialogue and discussion. They are somewhat alike, and in tandem they have a marvelous synergy. Unfortunately, most people lose out on this synergy because they fail to differentiate the two types of converse.

It may help in distinguishing them to recognize that discussion has the same root as percussion and concussion. This suggests something like a Ping Pong game in which the little white plastic ball is batted back and forth across the green table. Discussion is a type of human conversation in which we express our ideas about some common topic. For example, we have a discussion on "tracking." The members debate hotly the merits and demerits of this practice in the schools. The subject is dissected and analyzed from many points of view. We can learn a lot in such a discussion. The purpose of a discussion is to express your opinions in such a way that you can convince the others and win the game. Discussion is contentious, litigious, combative by nature. You may accept part of another discussant's view to strengthen your own argument, but the real purpose is not to capitulate but to conquer. There are a lot more discussions and debates going on today than there are dialogues. As good as discussions can be, and they are very helpful at times, they are only one wing for the bird. The other necessary wing is dialogue.

By contrast with discussion, the word dialogue comes from the Greek, *dialogos. Dia* means through. *Logos* means the word or, as some people say, meaning. It indicates that in a dialogue, meaning is passing through or moving through. In a dialogue, we say there is some movement when the dialoguing members consider the ideas of each other and use them to measure and test their own ideas. Since people change their minds in a good dialogue, we can see why it is indispensable in a Learning Organization.

In dialogue, we have the possibility of becoming observers of our own thinking. I have never met a truly educated person who wasn't a good observer of his or her own thinking. Put simply, I find most educated and highly cultivated people are enthusiastic about participating in dialogues. They know that dialogues sharpen and deepen their thought. A school should be a place where discussion and dialogue are an every day occurrence. Most of the other work should be done in preparation for the discussions and the dialogues. For example, the questions for reflection at the end of each chapter in this book are meant to be topics for such dialogues.

The awakened principal of a school now functioning as a Learning Organization, will rejoice that the stakeholders are using every opportunity to build teamwork through discussion and dialogue. The Shared Vision and values will be the subject of much of this conversation, and the members will feel empowered because their input actually influences the direction the school is taking. Mental Models and "mental maps" will never get outmoded in such a school because the dialogues will serve to keep our thinking more coherent and consistent. The principal will provide for dialogue as often as is feasible, and try to see that all participants are learning to "suspend" their assumptions, to literally hold them out in front of themselves. They will accept the criticism that comes in the discussion and the "light" that comes in the dialogue. In this way, they get these assumptions to more closely approximate what is true and real. The principal will model how important it is that each stakeholder (students included) be regarded as a colleague. Dialogues are empowering to all. The Learning Organization school makes it possible for all stakeholders to engage in this type of intellectual conversation.

SUMMATION

In this chapter, I outlined the dimensions of a Learning Organization and tried to show the roles played by Vision and Values, Dialogue and Discusssion in forming and maintaining such an organization. In Chapter 7, we will treat the Learning Organization from a different angle. We ask how the principal makes sure that things get done? In reply, we discuss the principal's use of time and energy, meetings, and the setting of plans into motion.

QUESTIONS FOR REFLECTION

1. Of all the changes our Rip Van Principal noticed after coming back to the principalship 20 years later, which ones did he find the hardest to cope with? Why?

2. If you were that Rip Van Principal returning after 20 years, what would you do first? Second? Third?

3. In this chapter, I use material taken from experts in the field of corporate management. Drucker, Deming, Senge, and Covey direct their remarks to the private sector. How can their teachings be applied to schools? Can what they mean by a Learning Organization fit a school?

4. Reflect on the definition of Organizational Oversight from *Principals For Our Changing Schools,* and see why it would fit a bank or construction company as well as it does a school. Why?

5. The first mark of a Learning Organization is that all the stakeholders are learners. Learning entails metanoia—a deep changing of the mind. Why must schools do more than disseminate information?

6. How do Vision and Values play reciprocal roles in the formation of a Learning Organization?

7. Which comes first in leading an organization—Values or Vision? Are they Mental Models?

8. How are dialogue and discussion alike? How are they different? Why are they indispensable in a Learning Organization?

9. No Learning Organization can exist without Shared Vision, Mental Models, and Team Learning. True or false? Why?

7

MAKING THINGS HAPPEN— IMPLEMENTATION

Management is not being brilliant.
Management is being conscientious.
Beware the genius manager.
Management is doing a few simple things and doing them well.
Peter F. Drucker

It isn't enough that our awakened principal has formed the stakeholders into a Learning Organization. The leader never abrogates his or her responsibility for implementing the plans which have developed from the Shared Vision. With all the dialogue and cooperative actions between stakeholders, the principal is still the leader and must see to it that the goals of the school are implemented. The vision statement needs to be put into operation and here we call on further leadership skills from the principal. How can principals be sure that the students are being given a quality education? No matter how empowered the stakeholders are, the school must be judged by its output. The principals not only take part in setting the plans in motion, they coordinate activities, monitor progress, support and encourage, and finally reassess the process to make certain

that all programs are moving in the direction indicated by the
Shared Vision. Even the latest management theories which
stress decentralized power and wide empowerment never
imply that the principal's role is confined to the front end of
the process. Cynthia McCauley and her team from North
Carolina have covered Implementation well in *Principals for Our
Changing Schools* in Domain 6 (13). I encourage you to read their
chapter with its clear definition and helpful process model. I
offer some supplementary material on leverage from the book,
High Output Management, by Andrew S. Grove. Linton Deck, a
member of McCauley's development team, is a colleague of
mine who shares my enthusiasm for Grove's approach to
Implementation.

SMART PRINCIPALS USE LEVERAGE IN LEADING

If you ask a group of principals what their output is, you
will get a variety of responses, but most will include the
following: judgments and opinions, directions, allocation of
resources, mistakes detected, staff trained, programs planned,
commitments negotiated, complaints handled, communications
with central office, programs assessed, staff motivated, public
informed, parents consulted, students counseled and
disciplined.

Do these really constitute the output of a principal? Not
really. They are, instead, activities, or descriptions of what
principals do as they try to produce a final result or output.
What, then, is a principal's output? The output for a principal
of an elementary school is a group of students who are ready
to successfully continue their education in the middle school.
The output of a principal in a middle school is, likewise, a class
of adolescents who are prepared to successfully continue their
education in the high school. The principal of a high school
should be concerned that all of his or her graduates are
prepared and motivated to go on learning, either through more
formal schooling or through on-the-job training after
graduation. Each of the three levels of schooling have a
mandate to help young people develop the basic skills and
knowledge which will equip them for the next stage of
education. A principal's output is flawed if the students who

leave or graduate have not developed a life-long love of learning, a basic belief in their own capacity to learn, and a realization that they are responsible for their own education.

If one thing is clear in our country today, it is that there is no place in the job market for high school graduates who don't further their formal education. The days of the blue collar worker are numbered. What we are observing is the obsolescence of an entire class of workers: the industrious but modestly educated man or woman for whom a factory job meant economic security. America is joining the new global economy which makes it imperative that we create pathways for all people to get good jobs. If we don't, unskilled workers will try to preserve the past, and our country will be the loser in global economic competition. The answer is simple. Every youngster in this country must get as much education as is possible.

If what we say is true, it makes eminent sense that awakened principals will use their powers in the most efficient way to assure a proper education of all students. This will entail using leverage. Principals can do their job, their individual work, and do it well, but that does not constitute their output. You can have a good principal and not have a good school. The principals' output must be measured by the output created by the stakeholders. It isn't what you do yourself that counts, it is what you get done through other people.

The principal performs countless activities necessary to produce the outcome. Not all the activities are of equal value, some are much more important than others. Good principals can keep many balls in the air at the same time. Great principals select the more important ones and juggle them expertly. The great principals must choose the activities with the greatest leverage.

How can a principal choose those activities which will do most to increase the quality and quantity of the school's output? The greater the output generated by any activity, the higher leverage power that activity has. These are the activities that the principal should be spending his or her time on. For every activity the principal performs, the output of the school should increase by some degree. Great principals have the knack of choosing those activities with the most leverage. They are sensitive to the leverage of what they are doing. Most principals I know (and I know over 2,000) work too hard. The secret of helping principals to increase school output is not getting them to work harder. It is in getting them to work smarter. The best way for working smarter is grasping this concept of leverage.

Principals' efficiency and productivity can be increased in four ways. In other words principals can improve their school's output in four ways:

1. Principals can increase the rate by which they perform their activities. They work faster.
2. Principals can increase the number of activities they perform. Work more hours.
3. Principals can increase leverage associated with various activities. They choose better.
4. Principals can enrich their mix of activities by choosing more activities with high leverage potential and fewer activities with low leverage. They work smarter.

I have no intention of giving you a list of what I think are the most leveraged activities you should use. That would be absurd and arrogant on my part. The activities you choose on any given day will be determined by many factors. I hope the most important consideration will be their leverage value. Each principal has his or her own style of leadership. Each school has different exigencies. The time of day, the political climate, the money available, the morale of the school, the rank of the school, parents' cooperation or lack thereof, the demographics of the school population, the bus service, and a thousand other factors play a role. Recognizing all the idiosyncratic aspects of principals' activity choices, it still makes sense for a principal to choose those activities which will do most to increase the quality and quantity of school output. It is as simple as that. Schools with rewarding outcomes have principals who choose highly leveraged activities.

Highly leveraged activities have three things in common: First, the principal's activity affects many stakeholders. Second, a brief, well focused set of words or actions by the principal has a long lasting affect on one of the stakeholder's activities. Third, the principal supplies a key piece of knowledge, skill, or information to a large group of stakeholders.

To illustrate the first law of leveraged activity, I will use the example of a meeting of all the personnel in a small rural school district. The superintendent, in this case, arranged for a morning session in which all 400 employees of his system would meet. I was privileged to do a workshop on school renewal. I reviewed the 12 principles of school renewal. The session lasted about 2 hours and seemed to go well. At the end, the superintendent graciously thanked me and took 15 minutes to perform a highly leverage activity. Speaking to all the stakeholders in his school system, after they had just been exposed to a workshop on renewal, he briefly reviewed the 12 principles we had covered, and then, showing his great leadership skill, he spelled out very simply, clearly, and concretely the three principles he felt should have highest priority. He offered a couple of nudges or directions under each area, and made it clear that he would cooperate with all the stakeholders in their efforts for renewal. Only the leader can give a charge to the team members. I, as an outsider, could offer help, but only the superintendent could give direction to the group. When principals have a chance to talk to all the stakeholders in the school these few minutes are precious. This is an activity of high leverage.

A good example of the second type of leveraged activity could be the performance review the principal conducts with each teacher twice a year. Just as the superintendent in the example above had to prepare well for the short talk he gave at the end of the workshop, so the principal has to prepare well for the performance review. Many principals have no idea how important and high leveraged are the moments they spend in doing their reviews. If I had one area in which I would encourage principals to improve their skills, it would be in doing these reviews. In another projected book, I plan to devote a chapter to the interviewing skills needed by principals.

In the third kind of highly leveraged managerial activity, the principal delivers, or gets someone else to deliver, some unique pieces of knowledge, or in some cases new skills or technical advances which can influence the work of the large group. Here the secret is to offer some specific help to a large segment of the stakeholders which will enhance the way they carry on their ordinary activities. An example would be to have someone come to the school and teach the seminar method to the teachers. Or have the principal himself or herself review with the staff some ideas on Outcome-Based Education, or on coaching, or block scheduling, etc. Note the principal should mandate the activity, but the principal doesn't necessarily deliver the unique pieces of knowledge or skills. For instance, I have been impressed by a Peer Coaching Method used in North Carolina, in which lead teachers are selected because of their acknowledged teaching skills, and they, in turn, coach other teachers. The lead teachers assist their assigned teachers with writing self-directed goals aimed at the refinement of instruction. The lead teachers meet with their assigned teachers throughout the year and use every possible means to help the teachers improve their teaching skills. In this third type of leveraged activity, the principal is choosing activities which will have long-lasting effects on groups of stakeholders. The time the principal spends in this way is golden because it affects groups of people at a deep level, and makes possible widespread and long-lasting improvement in the output of the school.

In any enterprise which involves developing youngsters, one can never assume that the plans will go smoothly and never need reshaping. What can go wrong usually does go wrong and the principal has to be around when damage control is called for. The real problem for most principals is that the problem solving or fire fighting takes up so much of their time, they don't get a chance to choose the higher leveraged actions whose main goal is the prevention of these fires. There is no substitute for skills in scheduling, monitoring, coordinating, and assessing. The principal can't just choose highly leveraged activities, he or she must try to enrich the mix between higher and less highly leveraged activities. The ratio is difficult to calculate but a rule of thumb might help. The 80–20 law says 20% of the day's activities call for damage control but it takes 80% of the time to handle this process. Ideally, we should spend 80% of the time preventing damage and only 20% in damage control. This leads us to a most controversial area—meetings. Are they a waste of time? Can we do without them? Which kind is most helpful? If you are like most of the principals I know, the word "meeting" has begun to make your hair rise and skin crawl. Meetings are what keep us from doing what we already know how to do.

MEETINGS CAN BE HIGH LEVERAGE OR LOW LEVERAGE ACTIVITIES

A friend of mine loves to characterize meetings as a time in which, after all is said and done, much more is said than done. There is a groundswell opposition to meetings in the school world these days because we have been deluged by them since the Carnegie Commission published *A Nation At Risk* in 1983.

Principals spend too large a segment of their available time in meetings that don't go anywhere, and yet it is absurd to think that a principal can lead a Learning Organization without meetings. Ideally, a principal should spend less than 25% of his or her time in meetings. One of the key responsibilities of a principal is to supply information and know-how, and to impart a sense of the preferred method of handling things to the stakeholders. This is what the superintendent did at that workshop I referred to earlier. He told the stakeholders to go on with renewal. He named three areas to start on and nudged them in a certain direction in pursuing the goals. A principal makes decisions and helps others to make decisions. Neither of these activities can be accomplished unless there are face-to-face meetings between the principal and the stakeholders. So meetings are essential. They are the medium through which the principal carries on his or her leadership functions. We can't fight meetings; instead we have to learn to use them in the most efficient or leveraged way possible.

PROVIDENT MEETINGS

The two roles of the principal produce the two basic kinds of meetings. In the first type of meeting, which we call *Provident Meetings*, knowledge is shared and information is exchanged. There is a real effort to clarify the Shared Vision and articulate the school mission and culture more clearly. Such meetings should take place on a regularly scheduled basis, but there is a real temptation to cut these meeting short or to avoid them all together. The second kind of meeting we call *Damage Control Meetings*. Meetings of this second type usually produce a decision. They are *ad hoc* affairs not scheduled far in advance, but, rather, called as a result of some problem which seems to interfere with the normal process. There is no way of avoiding this type of meeting, but the ideal is to keep them at a minimum and cut the finger pointing so often a part of them.

We call the first type of meeting "Provident Meetings" because their thrust is toward the future. They aim at avoiding problems, rather than solving, them. They help the stakeholders to look together into the future and share the vision. There are two kinds of Provident Meetings: "one on one" meetings like performance reviews, and, second, what used to be called staff meetings, but which I prefer to call Learning Organization Meetings. Both are initiated by the principal and scheduled far in advance. Such meetings can also be requested by individuals or groups.

I am indebted to Andrew Grove for many good ideas. It is his opinion that much of the success of his company, Intel, resulted from regularly scheduled Provident Meetings which were seriously planned and well-conducted. Provident Meetings deal with future-oriented topics and their aim is to recreate the organization. Many find that a 90 minute Provident Meeting held once a month keeps the Shared Vision alive and stimulates creative thinking. The participants dialogue and often leave with more questions than answers, but they leave thinking. Few companies or schools actually use this type of meeting. All genuine Learning Organizations use them faithfully.

DAMAGE CONTROL MEETINGS

Unlike the Provident Meetings which are regularly scheduled and anticipated over the year, the Damage Control Meetings are usually held *ad hoc* and are designed to produce a specific output, not infrequently an operational decision of the damage control variety.

One of the major problems in educational administration is that we are spending too much time on Damage Control Meetings and too little on Provident Meetings. A good goal to aim for would be to cut the time on the necessity for Damage Control, and increase it on Provident Meetings. In no case should we spend our whole meeting time on Damage Control. Of all the skills and knowledge that a principal could use in creating and maintaining a Learning Organization, the skill in planning and executing meetings of all types would have to rate among the top five.

FROM THE SUN'S SHADOW TO NANOSECONDS IN 500 YEARS

This chapter is aimed at helping principals make things happen. One of the most important parts of making things happen is to make them happen in a timely fashion. To throw a man a rope 10 minutes after he has drowned is not the way to do things. Just as principals have to learn the skill of conducting meetings and interviewing, they also need help in "timing." We live in a fast paced world. We now measure things in nanoseconds—one billionth of a second.

How has this speeding up of our perception of time affected schools? In most schools, a premium is placed on how fast we can recite an answer or solve a problem. No educator comes out explicitly claiming that intelligence and speed go together, but the whole system rests on that false assumption. By fourth grade some really deep thinkers are shunted aside because they worked at a snail's pace. They were not rewarded for pondering, reflecting, and musing. There is no time for the fourth type of thinking we discussed earlier. Testing has over utilized the stop watch.

One of the prophets of modern work was Frederick W. Taylor, and the stop watch was his bible. He was the first, and most influential, of a tribe of efficiency experts who came into prominence in the 19th century in the U.S. Their influence was gigantic and still determines much of how we work in schools and in the business world. He stamped a whole civilization with his "time neurosis." The schools followed the procedures of the textile factories.

Taylor called his process "Time Study" and clocked everything in sight. What Taylor did (and we are still trying to free ourselves from it) was to split each job into its component operations, and take the time of each part. This is the whole idea of scientific management. It is the systematic analysis and breakdown of work into its smallest mechanical components and the arrangement of these elements into the most efficient combination. Every detail of the man's job was specified. It has taken us a century to discover how wrong Taylor was. Talk about Barbara Tuchman's *March of Folly*, it would be hard to find a better example of it than Taylor's folly. How much of this has rubbed off on the schools?

We know for certain we cannot create a Learning Organization by following the mechanized approach of Taylor. Before General Motors awakened and discovered the philosophy used in their Saturn plant, they contracted with their workers on a 6 minute basis. For payroll calculations they divided the hour into 10 "6-minute periods," and the worker was paid by the number of tenths of an hour he worked. Are there any resemblances between the textile mill, the automobile production line, and the modern school as far as units of time are concerned? The principal will make things happen only if he or she learns how to use time in the service of the stakeholders. Until recently, we made the stakeholders serve time, rather than the reverse.

Businesses are learning that their employees enjoy flextime. At first, the employers' reaction was dubious, but now the employers agree that although it does add somewhat to costs, it is balanced by higher worker morale, less absenteeism, and less sick leave. Are there some things that principals could do to modify the clock as far as the stakeholders in a school are concerned? In the school system nearest to where I live, they are changing the morning arrival times for the elementary, middle, and high schools so that fewer new school buses will have to be bought. With this flexibility, each bus will be able to serve 75 students, whereas with the fixed morning arrival time, each bus could only serve an average of 50 students. This means one-third less buses in service, more hours of work for the school bus drivers, fringe benefits for bus drivers, and less driver turnover.

Year-Round Schools have proliferated in North Carolina, from 8 to 90 in 3 years. Principals of Year-Round Schools tell me they have more flexibility in the use of time. It helps teachers teach better and students learn better. The new morning schedule for buses also helps learning. Block scheduling will help in some subjects. If we wonder whether a time change is good or bad we just ask this question. "Does the change increase the probability of better learning on the part of the students and better teaching by the teachers?"

I am afraid we have been putting the cart before the horse. Time has been the master and learning the servant. Now principals have the opportunity to enrich the educational mix, organizing the teaching and learning process so that time is a function of learning and not the reverse. In this chapter, we are trying to help principals make things happen. It may be that principals can make things happen best by controlling the way time is used.

Let me give you a simple example. If you agree with me that staff development is one of the key elements in developing a Learning Organization, how could we push staff development into a late afternoon time slot when the teachers are dead tired after a taxing day's work? Why do we persist in trying to schedule PTA meetings for working parents after their days's work is done?

The Learning Organization teaches us that the high tech world of clocks and schedules, computers and programs which were supposed to free us from a life of toil and deprivation, has, instead, enslaved, exploited, and victimized many of us. We may have sped ourselves out of the time world of nature-sunrise, high noon, eventide, dusk, and sunset, and into a man-made world of nanoseconds in which we don't have time to experience, savor, and celebrate the gifts around us. If a Martian could observe a typical school in action, he or she would say, "They look like little ants on an ant hill running frantically in response to a series of bells and announcements over loudspeakers. No one has time to think, relate, reflect, or dialogue." I would have to agree. When I visit a school I am often appalled by the frenetic pace. School reminds me of that old TV program, "Beat the Clock." The reevaluation of time is a prerequisite to the renewal of a school. The wise principal will step back and see if there are not more humane ways to control school time. If we continue to be slaves of small segments of time we won't have big ideas.

DUAL REPORTING IS THE RULE, NOT THE EXCEPTION, IN A LEARNING ORGANIZATION

Another help for the principal in making things happen is the practice of Dual Reporting. As long as we had the bureaucratic model for a school, we thought of the principal as having a wide span of control in which all the stakeholders were directly responsible to the principal. Everyone reported to the principal, and the principal was the supervisor of all the stakeholders. In our mythical middle school, the principal would be responsible for the work of 1,000 students and 100 adult employees. It may have worked when the principal was only a straw boss communicating to the stakeholders decisions made by the superintendent. That becomes impossible when the principal is the leader of a team of professionals, who are charged not only with managing the operation but, more importantly, recreating the school. Remember, in our concept of the school as a Learning Organization, every stakeholder is learning and shares responsibility for the quality and quantity of schooling. The students themselves must learn that they are not only responsible for their own learning, they are also responsible for the climate of the school which influences the learning of all the other students.

With the advent of site management and the mandate to renew schools, principals have to learn a new style of management which incorporates the idea of dual reporting. In this new approach, a stakeholder can have more than one person to whom they report and are accountable. To understand dual reporting we have to explain that all true Learning Organizations are hybrid in form. Unlike the old style organization we were used to, this new form includes two strains or two forms—one is mission-oriented, the other function-oriented.

Put simply, the Learning Organization has a regular structure similar to the old type organization. The principal is still the chief and it is his or her responsibility to make sure the mission is accomplished. The function orientation is the new part. When Goodlad talks about groups of worriers in a school, he is referring to groups of stakeholders who are commissioned by the principal to look after some one or more of the commonplaces of schooling. The members of this group—let's call it the "Instructional Improvement Group"—work under the direction of the principal, but they are given great flexibility, autonomy, and authority in the area of instructional skills. Teachers who are being coached by the "Instructional Improvement Group" do dual reporting. As regular stakeholders in the school they report to the principal as their CEO, but they also report to the chair and members of the "Instructional Improvement Group." Note the "Instructional Improvement Group" cuts across other operational boundaries. In a high school, members of the Social Studies and Science departments may be reporting to members of the "Instructional Improvement Group," who are English or Art teachers.

The most important task a Learning Organization has is the optimum and timely allocation of its resources, and the efficient resolution of conflicts arising over that allocation. The mission of the Learning Organization is clear-—the improved learning of the students and all stakeholders. How can this best be done? Many, today, believe this can best be done by creating a hybrid organization in which all members learn to do dual reporting. The functional groups or groups of worriers in the words of Goodlad, function like groups of internal consultants who have a job to do in the organization and have the freedom to carry out their work without constantly taking direction from the principal. All members accept the fact that they will, at times, have two masters. This is matrix management and it appears to be the best way to make thing happen in our complex and changing organizations.

Perhaps an example may help to clarify the concept. Cecilia Greaney has been asked to become principal of Central High School. Only 36 years of age, she was teacher of the year during her third year of teaching Social Studies at Central High School. She has been a most successful head of the Social Studies Department for the last 4 years.

Cecilia was convinced that the High School needed a drastic change in leadership style. She was fearful that her ideas might be considered too far out and too threatening. When she ran the Social Studies department she supervised a teacher with a Ph.D. from Brown University, who was brilliant and had some great ideas about improving instruction using an interdisciplinary approach. "He helped me more than you will ever know," she said. At first Cecilia was intimidated, then she began to understand that this Social Studies teacher really liked high school age students, and had much to offer them as a teacher. He had no interest at all in becoming head of the Social Studies department. He didn't want to be an assistant principal or principal, but he did want to change the school into a Learning Organization. He was a scholarly teacher who brought out the best in the brightest students and still reached out to the average and below average ones. He wanted to get the other teachers to dialogue across department lines in order to enrich themselves and improve their teaching. Now he headed the "Instructional Improvement Group" and helped Cecilia to model the way a principal can set up dual reporting to utilize talents which before were wasted.

To put a man on the moon, NASA had to ask several major contractors, and many subcontractors, to work together, each on a different aspect of the problem. It was a gigantic project. Today, as I write, we are commemorating the 30th anniversary of the assassination of JFK. It is a sad day. If you are 40 years old or older, you certainly remember exactly where you were and what you were doing when you heard the president had been shot and killed. John F. Kennedy was the president, who in one of the darker moments of our nation's history, promised that we Americans would have a man on the moon by the end of the decade. He died before it occurred, but his promise was fulfilled. We had a man on the moon before the decade ended. "A small step for man, a giant step for mankind." This is a classic example of a Shared Vision which captivated a whole nation. NASA was given this charge and helped us discover a whole new way to accomplish the most complex of tasks using matrix management and dual reporting.

Cecilia and I talked about this historical event. How do you manage getting a man on the moon? If she were to accept the principalship at Central High, how could she use matrix management and dual reporting? How could she get some of the gifted teachers, like her Brown University Ph.D., to have much more influence in the school's future? How could she create a Learning Organization in which the more formal bureaucratic management structures would no longer function as hindrances to progress? These were exciting meetings. Cecilia was definitely ready to be a new style leader, but she had to forge ahead where there were no paths or maps to guide her. She wondered if she could do it. I had no doubt.

The whole idea of matrix management is rather simple. How could the leaders of NASA orchestrate the activities of all the contractors and subcontractors so that when problems developed in one place, they didn't necessarily subvert the whole process? In matrix management, resources can be diverted from a strong section to one that is slipping. The strong group would pitch in with the weaker one and help them make up lost time. This couldn't be done in the old style hierarchical model. Cecilia is among the young principals who are revolutionizing schooling. She makes things happen using dual reporting and matrix management.

LIVING UNDER TOO MUCH CONTROL LEADS TO LEARNED HELPLESSNESS

How does control play a part in implementing or making things happen? When we speak about the principal implementing the Shared Vision or bringing about the completion of the plans, it seems to imply that the principal is a powerful person who exerts a lot of outward control over the stakeholders who are doing the specific tasks. After all, we talk about the principal setting the plans in motion, coordinating activities, monitoring progress, supporting and encouraging workers, and, finally, reassessing. It certainly sounds like a boss standing on a platform overseeing the workers and making sure that by the wise use of his or her power the whole process is moving in the right direction. Understood in that way, the school is not a Learning Organization, but rather a tightly run factory run by one controlling boss. Earlier we talked about empowering the stakeholders, sharing not only vision but also power, and seeking to get the stakeholders themselves to take over the control of the process. A reasonable amount of control in the classroom is necessary. Too much control from the teacher will kill all learning. The same is true in a school. Control is necessary, but it should not come only from the top. The time has come for us to examine the idea of control and see to what extent it benefits or harms a Learning Organization.

A really fascinating psychological experiment was conducted at a nursing home. The experiment consisted of having the patients do 10-piece jigsaw puzzles. Seventy-two of the residents were considered capable of this activity, and this group was randomly assigned to three smaller groups. Group One was called the "Helped Group." In this group, at each of four 20-minute sessions, an examiner sat with the subject and encouraged him or her to work on the puzzle. Additionally, the examiner actively assisted in locating puzzle pieces, suggested where to put them, and often solved the puzzle with the subject. Group Two was called the "Encouraged Only Group." At each of four 20-minute sessions an examiner sat with the subject and instructed him or her to complete the puzzle, offering encouragement but only minimal assistance. Finally, Group Three, called the "No Contact Group," had no contact with any examiner. Subjects in all three groups were given a pretest and post-test trial of puzzle assembly performance by an assistant, who didn't know to which group they were assigned. Additionally, a post-test of self-confidence was administered to all the subjects.

Although the 72 residents were carefully matched and nearly identical at the start of the experiment, by the end of the experiment there were significant differences among the groups. As you might expect, the "Helped Group" performed less well than those in the "Encouraged Only Group," or those in the "No Contact Group." The "No Contact Group" did better than the "Helped Group," but not as well as the "Encouraged Only Group." The "Helped Group" scored lowest on the post-test measuring self-confidence and also scored worst on the test measuring the perception of task difficulty. Feeling little self-confidence, members of the "Helped Group" perceived the jigsaw puzzles as quite difficult.

Now apply what we have just learned to a school setting. Cecilia Greaney found herself principal of a high school in which the stakeholders did their daily jobs but felt totally helpless as far as changing the school itself. If Cecilia did not introduce matrix management and dual reporting, she would have an institution in which she and her two assistant principals would make all the decisions and take sole responsibility for planning and implementation. There would be no question of a Shared Vision. This would be a poor institution of learning rather than a Learning Organization. If a critical mass of stakeholders are not engaged in meaningful discussion and dialogue concerning the future of the school, then the school is not accomplishing its goals. Only when a majority of the stakeholders feel empowered and committed to the Shared Vision will they practice the five disciplines required by a Learning Organization.

THE PRINCIPAL MUST JUDGE TASK RELEVANT MATURITY

Andrew S. Grove, in his book, *High Output Management*, discusses task relevant maturity. It is an idea which could be helpful to principals. If in the case of Cecilia Greaney, we had assumed that everyone in the school would move forward at the same pace into creative ways of thinking and coping, we would have made a poor assumption. Each stakeholder has a different pace. Some are ready for any change, others are true laggards.

It is the job of the principal to assess how much change this or that stakeholder is capable of handling. If the principal is going to use leverage in changing a school into a Learning Organization, he or she will need to know how "task mature" each stakeholder is when it comes to initiating and accepting change. In determining how much time and attention a manager should give to each of his employees, Grove assumes those employees who have greater task-relevant maturity will need less of the manager's attention. Actually, this is the way it works in most schools. The principal pays least attention to the stakeholders who do their jobs in a responsible way. Good teachers don't need as much intervention, supervision, and training time as do those who have less task-relevant maturity.

We are not talking here about the stakeholders doing their jobs well, but rather about their tolerance for change in the whole system. I find it helpful to divide the stakeholders into five groups based on their readiness for change: the front runners, the early adopters, the early majority, the late majority and, finally, the laggards. In 1969, A. Mitchell, working at the Stanford Research Institute in California produced a marketing study, *American Values*, in which he and his associates discovered these five groups of innovative types. I have adapted them for principals and used them over the last 25 years. They seem to apply well to school stakeholders A wise principal is able to see into which groups his or her stakeholders fit. This is important if the principal is to use leverage in bringing major changes to the school.

◆ The *Front Runners*, who make up only 2.5% of the stakeholders, are a venturesome group. They are eager to try new ideas. They are often, but not always, made up of the youngest teachers and other staff. They like to apply complex technical knowledge to problems. Most are very good with computers. They like to take chances. The more a thing is risky and rash the better they like it. They find it easy to tolerate loose ends. The principal can get many new ideas from this group and needs to spend little time priming them for change. Unfortunately, the majority of stake-holders are not easily persuaded by this group whom they tend to think of as somewhat "flaky."

◆ The *Early Adopters* make up 13.5% of the popu-lation and they are the dream group for the principal interested in implementing change. They are well-integrated into their communities and enjoy great respect from all the other stakeholders. Others look to this group for advice and information about what is happening, some preferring to talk with members of this group rather than the principal. This is the group that will contribute most to forming and implementing the Shared Vision. They are the yeast in the mass. They love the role they play in society as informal leaders. Many have turned down the suggestion that they should become principals. Their greatest contribution lies in their ability to decrease uncertainty about a new idea or program by adopting it themselves, and showing other, less courageous, stakeholders that it is really a good move. Principals should spend a lot of time with the Early Adopters, not because they need supervision but because they have so much to offer the principal and all the others.

◆ *The Early Majority* are the principal's most helpful group next to the Early Adopters. This group is important if for no other reason than its size. The members make up 34% of the population. They are deliberate as a group. They will adopt new ideas, but not without a lot of reflection. They cannot be easily swept off their feet. They seem to follow the advice of Alexander Pope who counseled, "Be not the first by which the new is tried. Nor the last to lay the old aside." They don't want to be leaders or Laggards. They take their lead from the Early Adopters and influence the Late Majority. They trust their friends in the Early Majority because they deem them to be deliberate and solid in their judgments. If, with the principal's leadership, the Front Runners, the Early Adopters, and the Early Majority get behind a new program, then 50% of the population will have bought in. Final success will depend on getting the Late Majority to come on board, because few programs can get airborne if there are 50% of the stakeholders who can't or won't buy into it. Serious change ultimately depends on getting the Late Majority to take the plunge.

◆ *The Late Majority* also comprises 34% of the population. This group adopts new ideas and programs cautiously. When the principal or the Front Runners try to persuade them, they often dig their feet in and become adamantly opposed to the innovation. They always wait to see what others are doing before they take the plunge. They are "show me's" and need a lot of pressure from the Early Adopters and the Early Majority before they are willing to make a change. They feel as if they have very limited resources, so they want almost all uncertainty removed before they risk giving up what they are doing to do something new and untried. They seem to have infinite patience and at times do some very creative foot dragging.

◆ The *Laggards* are the rock-ribbed traditionalists. They make up 16% of the population and, unfortunately, often consume a lion's share of the principal's time and attention. They are the last group in the school to adopt any change. Parochial in their outlook, they shy away from any leadership roles. Many of them walk close to the wall and have few social contacts in the school. They are often loners who feel anxiety when others propose innovations which might interrupt their daily routine. They live in the past. While the principal is trying to sell the idea of computer terminals in every class, the Laggards are bemoaning the fact that the ink-filled pen had to yield to the ballpoint. They decide the present problem simply by looking back to what was done before. It is a shame that this group can take so much out of principals. I have seen principals with real promise give up because of the constant nagging from Laggards whose tunnel vision made them incapable of grasping the Shared Vision.

THE FIVE DISCIPLINES OF A LEARNING ORGANIZATION

The discussion in the last two chapters has ben heavily influenced by Peter M. Senge's book, *The Fifth Discipline*. According to Senge, there are five disciplines which must be practiced by those who would build a Learning Organization. The five are Shared Vision, Personal Mastery, Mental Models, Team Learning, and Systems Thinking. Implicit in my thinking has been the idea that the principal who learns the nine domains and practices the five disciplines will be a most successful transformative leader, one who can form and maintain a genuine Learning Organization. Here is a brief description of the five disciplines.

PERSONAL MASTERY

People with a high level of Personal Mastery are able to consistently realize the results that matter most deeply to them. They make things happen in the sense that they approach their own life as an artist would approach a work of art. Their secret is a deep dedication to life-long learning. They develop their intrapersonal, as well as the interpersonal, intellectual and emotional competencies. They do this by continually clarifying and deepening their own personal vision. They learn to focus their energies, develop patience, and see reality more and more objectively. A Learning Organization can only form if it has a sufficient number of its members seriously practicing Personal Mastery. Personal Mastery is the spiritual foundation of any Learning Organization. A true Learning Organization aids its members to increase in Personal Mastery.

MENTAL MODELS

We have referred frequently to Mental Models and I think you already have a fairly clear idea what they are. They are deeply ingrained assumptions, generalizations, or even pictures or images that influence how we understand the world and how we take action. We are often unaware of these Mental Models in ourselves. To practice the discipline of working with Mental Models we must start by turning the mirror inward. We have to learn to surface these internal pictures, examine them and allow others to criticize them, and finally change them when appropriate. We have to have the courage to surface them and hold them rigorously to scrutiny. Without this discipline our Personal Mastery efforts fail, and we are unable to take part in a Shared Vision.

SHARED VISION

If there is one idea about leadership that has been around for centuries, it is Shared Vision. The principal is the key person in a Learning Organization because he or she has the capacity to hold a shared picture of the future the stakeholders seek to create. The principal somehow gets the other stakeholders to contribute to the vision, buy into it, and propagate it. The practice of Shared Vision involves the skills of unearthing and expressing the shared picture of the future. Good principals use metaphors to get across the vision in a way which reaches the head, the heart, and the hands. The stakeholders buying into the Shared Vision practice commitment and enrollment. They are no longer passive followers. They are on fire with the Shared Vision and dedicate themselves to its achievement. The members must have their personal vision jibe with the Shared Vision. They do this often through dialogue in which they surface their Mental Models for criticism and learn how to listen to others. Principals know how futile it is to try to dictate a vision to others. It's in the Learning Organization with stakeholders dialoguing with their peers that the principal will see the Learning Team buy into the Shared Vision. We mentioned earlier the marvelous transformations that become possible when this discipline of Shared Vision is fully practiced.

TEAM LEARNING

We know that teams can learn in sports and in the performing arts. We have seen the results of such learning. In science we know from Heisenberg that much of the creative work is done in teams. Now businesses are beginning to stress Team Learning. There has been a complete turnabout in the way automobiles are produced, moving from an assembly belt approach in which workers had individual responsibilities, they worked alone, never saw the finished product, and were never consulted about the design of the car or their working situation. The new plant producing Saturns is 180 degrees in the opposite direction. The stress is on Team Learning. Instead of the cars moving by the individual worker on a belt, the team moves around the car which is in the center and all workers interrelate as they find better ways to assemble their vehicle. When finished, the team rejoices and moves on to another whole car. It is working so well that we are becoming competitive with the Japanese and maybe even edging them out a bit.

We know now that to practice a discipline is to be a lifelong learner. You never arrive. The discipline of Team Learning starts with dialogue. This is the capacity of members of a team to suspend assumptions (Mental Models) and enter into genuine "thinking together." To the Greeks who invented the word, dialogue meant a free flowing of meaning through a group, allowing the group to discover insights which couldn't be attained individually. As we said earlier, dialogue differs from discussion which is more combative. Discussion means literally a heaving or throwing of ideas back and forth in an argumentative manner. Some win, some lose in a discussion; all win in a dialogue. Team Learning uses both types of conversation but we are rediscovering the lost art of dialogue, and it can make a great difference in schools and business.

SYSTEMS THINKING

In Chapter 10 we use Systems Thinking to examine the goals of curriculum. Senge's book, *The Fifth Discipline*, explains in depth all five disciplines, but, as its title indicates, it places highest value on the fifth discipline which is Systems Thinking. It is impossible to do justice to this concept in a brief summary fashion. In this book, I am constantly trying to convince you, as principals, to do Systems Thinking as you use the 21 domains of knowledge and skills in changing your schools into Learning Organizations.

Senge offers a great example of the need for Systems Thinking—a rainstorm. As the clouds mass and we notice the leaves twist around and face upward, we know it will soon rain. After the storm is over, we know the runoff will feed into groundwater miles away, and the sky will clear by tomorrow. All these events are separated in time and space, yet they are all connected within the same pattern. Each event influences the other events, even though some of these events are not immediately visible to us. We don't see the runoff feeding into the groundwater. We don't see the groundwater forming an aquifer which will flow into the ocean. Nor are we present later when the ocean water evaporates, rising to form another rain cloud. The individual events are parts of a whole and connect together to form a pattern. We can only understand the system of a rainstorm by contemplating the whole. Knowing the individual parts taken separately won't help us understand the whole pattern with its interdependencies. When principals learn to look at their schools as patterned wholes in which every one of the commonplaces of schooling and the 10 themes are seen as interdependent and interrelated parts flowing together to produce the whole, then they will have made a giant step toward changing their schools into Learning Organizations.

One reason it is so hard for principals to do Systems Thinking is because they are a part of the web themselves. They have to learn to handle Mental Models and work at Personal Mastery if they are to grasp the Systems Thinking approach. What all of us do in perceiving the organizations of which we are a part, is to take snapshots—we artificially stop the process—and get a sample of what is happening at a given moment. That is what the end of course tests do. That is what the annual performance appraisal does. Feedback from spot checks is necessary, but not sufficient, for the Systems Thinking approach. They are snapshots of a process which ought to be caught in an ongoing action by a camcorder. We solve our deepest recurring problems only when we do Systems Thinking and deal with the whole instead of the individual parts.

Systems Thinking is the antidote to the sense of helplessness which grips so many of us in the field of education. The complexity of the system often undermines our confidence and makes us want to throw up our hands saying, "Nothing I can do will make a bit of difference. The problem is the System." We forget that we are a part of that system. Systems Thinking is a discipline (life-long) for seeing the "structures" that underlie complex situations, and for discerning high from low leverage changes. Only by seeing wholes do we learn to foster health in organizations. To help us see these wholes, Systems Thinking offers a language that begins by restructuring how we think. "The beginning of wisdom is to call things by their right names," says the Chinese proverb.

SUMMATION

In this chapter, I summarized material on leverage and the five disciplines. Together these should help principals implement the Shared Vision. In the next chapter we will develop some ideas from domain #7 in *Principals for Our Changing Schools.* Ivan Muse, and his Utah group, offer some helpful ideas on delegation which will make it easier for principals to run Learning Organizations. I will argue that principals must not only delegate responsibility but also authority if they want a Learning Organization. Perhaps equally important will be the principal's investment in training the stakeholders in the disciplines of Personal Mastery and Team Learning. When the Utah team developed the dimensions of effective delegation they hit all the bases: task identification, identification of delegatees, authority and responsibility, support and feedback, participation and autonomy, accountability, and, finally, assessment. I will try to show how these essentials of delegation are best accomplished when the stakeholders are pursuing the disciplines of Personal Mastery and Team Learning.

QUESTIONS FOR REFLECTION

1. How would you differentiate the activities of a principal from the outcomes of a principal?

2. I make this statement in the chapter: "If one thing is clear in our country today, it is that there is no place in the job market for high school graduates who don't further their formal education." What does this mean for principals of K-12?

3. As a principal, how would you rank your activities, starting from the most and going to the least leveraged? What do highly leveraged activities have in common? Why?

4. How could a principal cutdown on Damage Control Meetings and increase Provident Meetings?

5. Give three glaring examples in your school in which time is the master and learning is the slave. How would you change scheduling so that time would be the servant and learning the master?

6. If Cecilia Greaney uses matrix management with dual reporting won't the stakeholders take advantage of the situation and shirk their obligations? After all, you can't serve two masters.

7. The "Helped Group" in the nursing home experiment did poorly because they were given the impression by staff that they couldn't do things on their own. The "Encouraged Only Group" did the best. Try to explain to someone why this conclusion can apply in a school setting.

8. In assigning your stakeholders to various roles, how could you improve the process by considering their "task-relevant maturity"?

9. Why should a principal spend more time with the Early Adopters? Why do principals spend so much time defending against the attacks of the Laggards? What would be a better approach?

10. Show how necessary it is to have stakeholders practicing all five disciplines if the school is to become a Learning Organization. Which discipline is easiest to understand? Hardest?

8

DELEGATION THROUGH DIALOGUE

The Learning Organization that performs together,
transforms together.

It isn't easy to delegate. Those of you who have had some experience as principals will agree that it takes courage to hand over both responsibility and authority to a stakeholder who has only moderate task-related maturity. Then why not delegate only to those who are perfectly capable of assuming responsibility? For the very good reason that such people are in short supply. The principals, themselves, are being handed responsibilities and authority they never had before, and they are trying to select stakeholders willing to take on more. This is the best of times and the worst of times as far as schooling is concerned. At no other time have principals and stakeholders been given the opportunity to reform and renew schools, while at no other time has budget cutting and blind criticism of schools been more forceful. It will be difficult to build the coalitions that will make it possible to renew schools under the present strained circumstances. If ever there was a time for the proper use of delegation, team learning, and dialogue, this is the time.

We are fortunate to have a clear description of delegation provided under Domain #7 in *Principals For Our Changing*

Schools. Ivan Muse, and his team from Utah, define delegation in a manner that allows for creative leadership.

> "Delegation: Assigning projects, tasks, and responsibilities together with clear authority to accomplish them in a timely and acceptable manner; utilizing subordinates effectively; following-up on delegated activities." (14)

They point out that organizations are created because one person acting alone cannot accomplish all that needs to be done. As schools get larger, the tasks they are called upon to accomplish become more numerous, complex, and critical to the well-being of all involved. I can't think of delegation these days without immediately thinking of Team Learning. In fact, I would dare to claim that a Learning Organization functions as a group whose interrelated learning makes it possible for the work to be shared at all levels. The key to improving delegation through Team Learning is improving dialogue, which empowers all team members. When thus empowered, the stakeholders can both give and take delegation. Taken together, these activities become the means for highly leveraged leadership by the principal.

THE PRINCIPAL AS DELEGATOR

Successful principals who have mastered the skills of delegating appear to share the following characteristics.

- ◆ They take a personal interest in each of the stakeholder's achievements.
- ◆ They take pride in the accomplishments of all the groups of stakeholders.
- ◆ They take time to help each group work to set work conditions.
- ◆ They constantly inform all groups and subgroups of the performance of the school as a whole and their groups in particular.
- ◆ They make a practice of giving credit to the groups who are handling delegated tasks.

- ◆ They make conscious efforts to motivate all stakeholders realizing that knowledge of results is one of the greatest motivators. They reward team efforts even when not fruitful.
- ◆ They make all stakeholders an integral part of school programs and decisions.
- ◆ They spend the lion's share of their time teaching and modelling Team Learning and dialogue.
- ◆ They make it known over and over again that a school's success depends on all the stakeholders being empowered through a shared vision to take responsibility even if it isn't explicitly delegated.

Muse and his associates offer some cautions on the use of delegation when deciding on the person or group to whom a task or responsibility should be given. They caution that principals should not:

- ◆ Give assignments to the same individuals because he or she is always willing to accept them;
- ◆ Give assignments that are too difficult and demanding for a particular individual or group;
- ◆ Give assignments to persons who are unwilling to accept responsibility for them;
- ◆ Give assignments without clearly explaining expectations and benefits of the task to the individual and the school; or
- ◆ Give assignments that tend to be routine and unchallenging.

Assigning duties is one of the main tasks of a principal. In a school, the principal must delegate major responsibilities to all the stakeholders. You, as principal of Mayberry Elementary School, assign the teaching of one section of third graders to Katherine Tortora. This is a major delegation. The 28 third graders in that section will be under the care and authority of Miss Tortora for a whole year. You can't go into that classroom and supervise every class that Miss Tortora teaches. You hand over responsibilities and authority to this young lady who has just graduated from college. You are fortunate if you get to pay a brief visit weekly or monthly. You delegate the responsibility of supervising her teaching to one of your lead teachers who has been chosen for the Peer Teaching Program. You also assign Katherine to lunch room duty. Each day, from 11:30AM until 12:10PM, she must keep order during the lunch period, and you assign to your assistant principal the responsibility of training and supervising the lunchroom work of Katherine Tortora. Katherine now reports to you as principal, to the assistant principal, to the lead teacher, and, incidentally, to the director of food service. It becomes apparent that principals are using delegation widely. It is impossible to run a school without delegating, but it is possible to run a school better if the principal becomes more skilled in delegating. The treatment of Delegation in *Principals For Our Changing Schools,* will be most helpful to all principals. I will briefly summarize it here.

Many of the principals I know complain that oftentimes teachers and others to whom they delegate drop the ball and make it necessary for them to do the task themselves. Some principals get burnt so often they stop delegating and put in 70–80 hour work weeks. This explains why so many principals are taking the first opportunity to retire. I listen sympathetically to their stories and I realize they are true for the most part. There is a real shortage of stakeholders who have task-relevant maturity and who are willing to assume added responsibilities. There are many stakeholders who feel no compunction about letting responsibilities slip without informing the principal. School renewal can only progress as we produce more stakeholders who are gaining task-relevant maturity and the willingness to go the extra mile.

On the other hand, some principals are so used to handling many responsibilities and to making decisions quickly, they often delegate but maintain tight control over tasks. Successful delegation depends on the principal's ability to assign responsibility and authority without excessive supervision and direction. Many stakeholders in today's schools want to be able to make suggestions and be taken seriously. They have been brought up in families in which they were allowed to inject ideas and express their uniqueness. Even though they may lack task-relevant maturity, they claim the only way they will get that maturity is with the experience of delegated responsibility and authority. I know from experience that this is true also. Many principals are so afraid to "let go," they never give the stakeholders the experience they need. Without this experience, they will never develop into real Learning Team members. In Learning Teams, one strong task-oriented group will perceive that another weaker group is struggling and they will pitch in and help. Only with stakeholders who are willing to take responsibility, principals willing to give it, and Learning Teams which take responsibility for more than their own precincts, can we build Learning Organizations. This will solve the delegation dilemma.

When I was young, if I asked to go ice skating, my mother would say, "It's too dangerous. You don't know how to ice skate. I don't want you ice skating until you know how." Of course, we all laughed and I asked her, "How can I ever know how (task-relevant maturity) if I don't go ice skating to learn how?" Her unfailing answer, "You'll never understand because you'll never be a mother." She was right on both scores. I never became a mother and I did learn how hard it is to let the young risk. Human nature is pretty consistent in this: those in authority find it hard to yield authority for a number of reasons.

The chapter on Delegation in *Principals For Our Changing Schools*, written by Muse and his team, offers a helpful diagram "Dimensions Of Effective Delegation" (15). It includes seven dimensions: task identification, identification of delegatees, authority and responsibility, support and feedback, participation and autonomy, accountability and assessment.

Under the heading Leverage, I discussed the first of these, and under Task-Relevant Maturity, the second. Now I want to make it clear that principals don't abrogate their own authority or take themselves out of the "loop" when they delegate a task. They have a responsibility to the delegatees to help them in any way possible to accomplish the task. The principal doesn't leave them hanging in the wind without support or feedback.

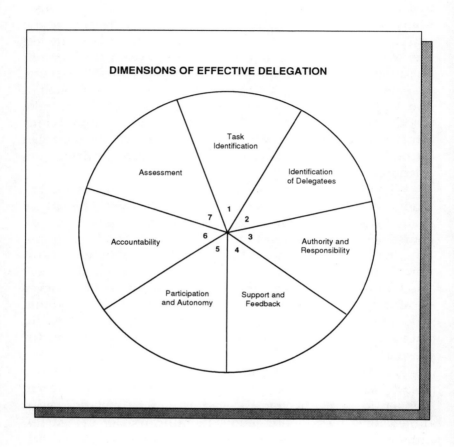

DIMENSIONS OF EFFECTIVE DELEGATION

Some principals forget how important it is to make a public announcement when they delegate. They should make it clear to all stakeholders that Abrams, Curry, D'Andrea, and Giggins have been appointed members of the Graduation Committee whose function it is to oversee the planning and execution of the graduation ceremonies. This public announcement makes it clear that anyone who has questions concerning graduation should confer with these committee members. Moreover, the stakeholders should not be surprised if they are contacted by one of these persons and asked to contribute their time and skills to the graduation ceremony.

Feedback may be an overused word these days but it is talked about more than it is utilized. It is amazing how often in schools the communication is flawed. Once the principal has delegated a task to an individual or a group, he or she is responsible for making sure that the delegatees are in the "loop" concerning information pertinent to their delegated responsibilities. For example, the principal gets a memo from the superintendent mandating that elementary school graduation ceremonies must be completed before 10:30PM. It is important that the principal make copies of the memo available to all members on the Graduation Committee. Teachers whose grades will have a bearing on who graduates should keep in contact with the Graduation Committee. Since the music department plays such an important role in the graduation ceremony, Miss Giggins, a music teacher, was appointed to the Graduation Committee. The principal lets it be known that although she is ultimately responsible for giving support and feedback to the Graduation Committee, she expects every stakeholder to cooperate.

If the Graduation Committee members need more time, the principal will try to release them from some other activities during the busy period before graduation. They need to know how the graduation budget is faring. Will the florist who gave us such a good price on the flowers last year be willing to do the same this year? Ask the school secretary. Her brother-in-law is the florist. Will the custodian be willing to use his truck again to move equipment? The principal must give sincere, positive, and frequent feedback to the committee. When the principal hears that a few parents are petitioning the superintendent to disallow caps and gowns at the ceremony, he makes this known immediately to the committee. Just as a principal hates to be blind-sided because some stakeholder failed to inform her of something for which she is responsible, the members of the Graduation Committee hate to be left out of the "loop." People don't want to look stupid because they don't know something they should have known. It is hard to exaggerate the importance of open communication in delegation. Support and feedback are the bread and butter of good delegation.

As for participation and autonomy, it is important to point out that participation should occur at two levels. The participation of the principal after the delegation has been made was discussed earlier. The delegatees also should be able to participate after the delegation has been made. They should have input into how and when tasks are to be completed. The delegatees should be involved in the decisionmaking process whenever possible. The Graduation Committee is not expected to follow last year's protocol to the last detail. Like any living tradition, the graduation will have many parts that are similar to previous graduations, but it will also have distinctively new elements that reflect the personality of the graduating class and the Graduation Committee. Only as these delegatees take responsibility and use authority will they gain in task-relevant maturity. Only when they gain in this maturity will the principal be able to delegate larger chunks of authority and responsibility, freeing her to do less and vision more. Now we have the start of a Learning Organization.

When the principal delegates a task, he or she makes sure that the delegatees agree to meet at regular intervals to review progress. The Graduation Committee was appointed in January. The principal arranged for a monthly breakfast meeting. There should be other *ad hoc* meetings as needed and the individuals should feel free to meet with the principal when necessary. The principal avoids telling the members how to do things, but she is not afraid to point out pitfalls. At these meetings, the principal praises the stakeholders and indicates her pleasure when she finds the planning and implementation going along on schedule. To ensure accountability, the types of information to be reported and the means for reporting should be specified before the Graduation Committee is empowered to act independently.

The last step in the process is assessment. After the graduation the principal is responsible for assessing the performance of the Graduation Committee. This review should focus on all stages of the process and provide for support and validation of the stakeholders' work. A principal who publicly praises the people who perform tasks well is always respected and revered. She is the type of principal who helps stakeholders to grow in task relevant maturity. The principal tells each of the committee members how grateful she is for their efforts and skills. She compliments them on the team learning that evolved. She lets them know that this experience with graduation will be good training for future delegated efforts. Perhaps most important, the principal asks for candid feedback from the Graduation Committee members relative to her role as the delegator. How could she have improved the process?

DELEGATION, DISCIPLINE, AND SELF-MASTERY

To this point we have been placing the primary responsibility for good delegation on the back of the principal. There is another side to this issue, the relative task maturity found among the stakeholders. A principal can only delegate if she has stakeholders with enough potential skill to be trained as Learning Team members. They must be willing and able to take delegation and to carry out complex tasks without minute supervision. Good principals seem to have stakeholders around them who can take delegation and carry through on responsibility. How do I know that? Goodlad makes it clear that those schools which were judged to be most satisfactory in his study of 38 schools, all had principals who shared one thing in common. They all claimed they had good stakeholders. Is this a coincidence or is there some underlying connection between good principals and good stakeholders? It is my belief that good principals both attract good stakeholders and create them by treating average stakeholders as if they were potential superstars. The first thing a good principal does, is model what it means to be a disciplined leader.

Principal Hughes has a fan club made up of the Early Adopters from his own school. They seem to radiate happiness when they meet with other teachers. They are not bashful in bragging about their school and principal. When good stakeholders in other schools get the message that Frank Hughes is a principal who is exciting to work with, many try to transfer to his school. These self-selected stakeholders who are motivated to renew the school are just what Frank Hughes needs.

Not all the stakeholders in Frank's school are ready to join teams in school renewal. He inherited a group of Laggards who make loud noises, and a Late Majority which is very hard to move forward. They are so afraid of making a mistake. When Frank brags on his staff he is not unaware of the fact that those helping him create a Learning Organization are still a minority. Frank is an optimist. He always treats the Laggards and Late Majority with respect.

Frank asks himself, "How can I get more of the stakeholders to buy into the Shared Vision and to learn the discipline of Personal Mastery?" They are afraid, not confident of, their coping skills. If only they had more Personal Mastery and could accept change better, then they would have the courage to influence their uncertain future. To do this they will need to pursue the discipline of Personal Mastery.

I have been using the word discipline without defining it. Like so many English words this one has a variety of meanings. To school people it usually has the connotation of behavior control. For example, we say the assistant principal is in charge of discipline. That means she must see to it that the students are under control at all times and are not allowed to disrupt the classrooms, corridors, cafeteria, etc. When Frank Hughes is thinking about engaging a wider range of his stakeholders in the pursuit of the discipline of Personal Mastery, he is using discipline in a very different way.

Frank is trying to build a Learning Organization. If this type organization was like an airplane or a computer then the components he used would be called "technologies." Instead, Frank is a social architect and he is building a special kind of organization. He is constructing some innovations in human behavior and the components in this case should be called "disciplines." A discipline in this context is a body of theory and skill that must be studied and put into practice. It is a developmental path for acquiring certain skills and competencies. Just as in learning to play the piano, some people have an innate gift, but most develop proficiency through practice. This meaning of discipline comes closer to the idea of disciplineship. To practice a discipline is to be a life-long learner. To practice a discipline is to be committed to life-long learning.

My professional discipline is clinical psychology. I have been practicing it for over 40 years. I would never dare say I had even come close to mastering it. Psychology, like any of the professions or trades, is growing and changing daily. Frank Hughes, the principal, is practicing the profession of school administrator. Like yourselves, he is constantly learning how to improve as a practicing principal. He knows that it will take a life dedicated to constant learning to stay ahead of the change curve.

Paderewski, the great Polish pianist, was quoted as saying, "If I don't practice for 2 weeks the audience will notice the difference in my performance. If I don't practice for a week the critics and my fellow musicians will notice. For myself, if I don't practice 5 hours every day, I will notice the difference."

When you practice the discipline of school administrator, you are more like an orchestra conductor than an individual performer. The conductor must not only practice conducting in his room, he must practice with the orchestra. Zubin Mehta, the conductor, required that the full New York Philharmonic Orchestra practice four times a week. Frank Hughes, the elementary school principal, is like a symphony conductor working with a full orchestra (all the school stakeholders), practicing incessantly until they get the school functioning like a Learning Organization. The Laggards in a symphony orchestra, who refuse to follow the direction of the conductor and insist on playing all the notes a half-beat slower than the rest, have a short tenure in the New York Philharmonic if they ever get there in the first place.

The elementary school principal finds himself in a predicament. He must delegate as the conductor does. It would be impossible for conductors to run around and play all the different instruments. You, as a principal, can't improve your performance unless you can get a sufficient number of the stakeholders to handle delegated responsibility and authority. Just as the viola players in a symphony must practice alone, as well as with the orchestra, so stakeholders in a school must pursue Personal Mastery on their own before they can take delegation and perform as a team member. It would seem obvious, that of all the professions, that of educator would be the clearest example of a profession in which the practitioners would need to continue honing their skills forever. Of all the professions this would be the one in which the need for daily practice and the pursuit of Personal Mastery would be most apparent.

As you can see, Frank Hughes has his work cut out for him. How can he get more of the stakeholders to pursue Personal Mastery so they will feel more comfortable with change? How can he get them to accept the delegated responsibility and authority for carrying out these changes? It isn't too late to get many of the Late Majority, and even some of the Laggards to opt for the discipline of Personal Mastery.

PERSONAL MASTERY

What is Personal Mastery? It might be best to define it by saying that people with a high level of Personal Mastery are able to consistently realize the results that mean most to them. They have goals and are able to accomplish these goals. These people approach their lives as an artist would approach a work of art. They take responsibility for their future and realize they are unfinished, and need constant improvement. Mistakes and errors don't devastate them. They can get off the canvas time and time again and still believe they are going to win the match. They are forever trying to fill in and smooth out their deficiencies. They do this by becoming committed to life-long learning.

When we pursue the discipline of Personal Mastery, we must continually clarify and deepen our personal visions, focus our energies, develop patience, and improve our ability to look at the world and ourselves objectively. These are essential steps in the process of becoming fully human. When we pursue the discipline of Personal Mastery, we are doing what we are called to do—become the best person we are capable of becoming.

Earlier in his career Frank went through a period during which he fought change. He wasn't ready at that time to risk giving up some of his routines and Mental Models. Now Frank has become a friend of change and a perfectionist like Fred Astaire. He is committed to continually seeing reality more accurately, just as Fred Astaire did when he worked so hard with Ginger Rogers to polish their dance routines. Ginger was dragged through countless repetitions until Fred was satisfied that they had it just right. Fred Astaire, like all pursuers of the discipline of Personal Mastery, saw reality so accurately he could spot flaws which everyone else missed including poor, tired Ginger Rogers. People who are pursuing the discipline of Personal Mastery are trying to do more perfectly what they choose to do and trying to choose more wisely what is worth doing. They want to choose what most fits their vision and do it as well as they can.

Once Frank Hughes started to pursue the discipline of Personal Mastery, he changed the way he perceived the world and his relations with it. He started to change the way he taught and even more the way he thought. When he was appointed a principal, his biggest problem was the realization that many of the stakeholders in his school had not yet opted to pursue the discipline of Personal Mastery.

TEAM LEARNING AND DIALOGUE LEAD TO PERSONAL MASTERY

Frank Hughes was in the midst of a discussion at PEP when he "saw the light." It is possible to come to major insights when we are alone. In fact, without sufficient time alone we are unable to practice Creative Thinking. That is the kind of thinking which makes it possible for us to change our minds, an important part of the learning process. Yet, it is impossible to create a Learning Organization unless the members are able to surface their Mental Models, examine them, and change them, which occurs most often in conversations with their peers. For this reason conversation consisting of discussion and dialogue is the prime means used in Team Learning.

Instead of moaning about the lack of task related maturity in some of his stakeholders, Frank saw it as his duty to help them gain Personal Mastery through Dialogue and Team Learning. To accomplish this, he needed to get some vehicle by which they could learn in small groups through the use of discussion and dialogue. Wouldn't it be great if all his stakeholders could have an experience away from school in which they might be able to learn how to dialogue better? He dreamed of having the 40 stakeholders go off together to the university for a weekend so they could experience what he had at PEP.

Frank canvassed the stakeholders; they liked the idea very much. Surprisingly, there was general agreement that it would be helpful if the school adopted an overarching, unifying theme like many of the magnet schools were doing. Three natural leaders in the group must have been talking together about it previously, because they all came up with the same idea, an International or Global Education school. Frank got permission, raised the money, and made arrangements with PEP staff for his stakeholders to attend a weekend workshop. A principal from a neighboring county with experience in Global Education volunteered to help them.

It became a reality 3 months later. They went to the university and spent a hard, but rewarding, weekend. The stakeholders broke up into small groups and discussed the pros and cons of having a unifying theme for their school. Frank's staff decided tentatively to plan the first steps in this shift to a Global School. Perhaps the two most important outcomes of the weekend workshop were their newly found ability to discuss and dialogue openly with each other on serious topics, and the beginning of a Shared Vision which seemed to unite and energize them. The talk went on far into the night. They went back home Sunday with tentative plans—a schedule of sub-group meetings which would include parents and students. That was the origin of the Global Education School I mentioned earlier in the book.

NO DIALOGUE NO TEAM LEARNING

With the advent of site management, principals are learning quickly that their "so called" power and autonomy is a myth unless their stakeholders are willing and able to take delegated responsibility and authority. The principals are aware, as never before, that it is impossible to force people who lack Personal Mastery to buy into a Shared Vision which demands changes. What is a principal to do? It appears to be a "catch-22." Most of the principals I know who are successfully leading the renewal of their schools have figured it out in this way:

- ◆ We have to get the stakeholders actively learning again.
- ◆ They will learn best if we can get them into small Learning Teams.
- ◆ In these small Learning Teams, they must experience dialogue and discussion in a positive way. Many have had little or no experience with education for judgment.
- ◆ Our hope is that if they start learning together they will buy into a Shared Vision.
- ◆ Whatever particular Shared Vision they choose (Global Education School) will be less important than the fact that the Shared Vision will create a Learning Organization.
- ◆ When they think about changing the whole school to realize their Shared Vision, they will see immediately that it can be accomplished only by Learning Teams accepting delegated responsibility and authority and cooperating in their planning and execution.

What I would like to do now is try to show principals that the first step in changing their schools into Learning Organizations could be as simple as introducing seminars into the program. Adler calls it the "Wednesday Revolution." The seminars would start with the principal conducting these groups with 12 to 15 adult stakeholders spending 90 minutes discussing some prearranged topic for which they have done some serious preparation. The next step would be training some of the stakeholders to become seminar leaders themselves. The eventual dream is that all stakeholders in the school could become capable of leading a seminar group. With the passage of time parents and students would also be integrated into the seminars. Then we would truly have the beginnings of a Learning Organization.

I will venture to say that we can't have Learning Teams without dialogue. In dialogue, a group explores complex, difficult issues from many points of view. Ideally, individuals suspend their assumptions (Mental Models) but they communicate these assumptions freely. The result is a free exploration that brings to the surface the full depth of one's experience and thought. It makes it possible for them to move beyond their individual views. It is the start of Team Learning. In the past, schools focused on the teacher teaching and the individual student learning. It will take us some time to appreciate the natural learning benefits that accrue from discussion and dialogue.

One advantage to dialogue is the way it helps us perceive the lack of coherence in our own thought. There are three ways that I tend to go off the track in dialogue. First, I realize that I am not talking about the same thing the other participants are. Instead, I am talking as if my Mental Model of the thing is the real one. Second, I catch myself going off the topic and thinking about how I wish things were, rather than listening to others to find out how they view the situation. I tend to be pollyanna like, and fail to see the difficulties involved. Lastly, my values intrude. For instance, I am forever assuming that every one is exactly like me in relishing quick changes and enjoying risk taking.

Without dialogue many of us never get the chance to change our minds, and make a better approximation of the real situation. Dialogue will set us free if we give it a chance. It is the only way we humans can grow and become all that we are capable of becoming. We were born to participate in the human conversation.

In dialogue with my peers, I find that I have been skipping logical steps and jumping at conclusions which I can't substantiate. Sometimes it hurts to realize how incoherent I can be, but it is worth it. I also discover in dialogue that I have some good insights which, with the help of other participants, I can flesh-out. The other participants help me find practical means to get my insights to work. It isn't pooled ignorance. It is pooled wisdom. It is exciting and contributes to my insatiable desire for life-long learning. Time seems to fly when we are engaged in a good dialogue.

The Principals' Executive Program has evolved over the last 10 years, and one of the marked changes involves the more frequent use of our limited class time for teaching the "Seminar Method." We now believe that this is the best use of precious time if we are interested in learning for understanding. At present, everyone in the class of 40 principals not only acts as a participant in three or four 90-minute seminars, each principal has the experience of directing a seminar and receiving a critique from colleagues. It is impossible to quantify the effects of this seminar teaching in the field. However, from anecdotal evidence I collect as I speak at different school systems, I am convinced that seminar work is one of the most powerful skills principals bring back to their schools from the PEP experience. Principals tell me that seminar teaching is working for them with faculty and students. All they need is the courage to use flexible scheduling so they can fit in seminars. These seminars are the first step in building Learning Teams. They start the "learning juices" flowing in many stakeholders who seemed "burned out."

THE ARTISTRY OF SEMINAR LEADERSHIP

Not only does the seminar give the stakeholders a feeling of empowerment, the dialogue helps them explore the depth of their thinking and experience. Seminars are the vehicles for gaining deeper understanding and appreciation of thoughts and feelings that we may have been acquainted with previously, but only in a superficial way. Adler never tires of telling us that the outcome of a Socratic seminar is a deeper understanding of ideas and issues. It is never confined to knowledge about a body of subject matter. In a seminar we aren't just looking for facts or information; rather, we are or should be involving ourselves in considering the significance of what we are discussing.

Suppose we were comparing and contrasting Hamlet and Othello in a seminar, and about 40 minutes into the dialogue one of the participants says, "I'd love to see the heroes switched. Let Hamlet be the general whom Iago is working on to bring out his jealousy, and let Othello be the prince whose father was murdered by his uncle and then married the prince's mother." Try to imagine how the dialogue might go in such a situation. It opens up all kinds of possibilities. One participant asks, "How would the plots of these plays be different if the lead characters were switched?" How do you readers think the plot would be changed? Close this book and think about it for a few minutes.

Assuming the participants in my example of the seminar on Hamlet and Othello had spent the necessary time reading both plays carefully and reflecting on them, they would be loaded with ideas about how this switch would influence the plot. Can you imagine Othello waffling and procrastinating like Hamlet, or would he dispatch the new king without waiting for any travelling players to "catch the conscience of the king?" Do you think Iago would have been as successful in deceiving Hamlet as he was with Othello, or would Hamlet have seen through the crude facade?

Assuming that reading Shakespeare's plays can be both entertaining and informative, can our deep study, reflection, and dialogue on Hamlet and Othello help us to understand human nature better? Can it help us not only experience a catharsis, which was Shakespeare's first aim, but also open a much deeper understanding of how people act in crisis situations? Could it help us understand ourselves and other people better? The answer is yes, and that would be true if we just read these two plays in solitude and never discussed them. However, when we have a group discussion of them, we are enabled to understand and appreciate them so much more deeply and fully. The comments of others help us see things we missed. As we express our insights to others, we begin to understand what we are saying better. The seminar experience is an essential tool for life-long learning. Only when Americans begin again to join into conversation on ideas of merit will our learning curve start to ascend. Seminars point the way.

One principal came to me after such a seminar experience and asked, "Why wasn't I given this opportunity during my 19 years of formal education and all the in-service training for the last 11 years?" He had been in school 30 years and never really experienced seminar learning. Countless principals have told me they were flabbergasted to think they could get so excited and involved in discussing the works of Machiavelli, Shakespeare, Martin Luther King, Jr., etc. I can remember a principal shaking his head and saying, "I'm an old football coach, I never thought I would be taking part in a seminar on Plato's *Crito* and enjoying, as well as understanding, it. Maybe I'm smarter than I thought I was." I'll let you in on a secret. There are thousands of principals out there who are a whole lot smarter than they think they are. They were short changed in their educations because all the emphasis from Kindergarten through Master's degree was on didactic instruction, following directions, memorizing, filling in blanks, answering true-false and multiple-choice tests as a goal, and they studied for objective tests with grades as a goal. They had been given little coaching after fourth grade. They never heard of the Socratic method of questioning, and they were never fortunate enough to be exposed to a real seminar. The Learning Organization school will demand teaching balance between didactic, coaching, and seminar.

The seminar always begins with questions. The hardest part of leading a seminar takes place before it starts when you strive to think up the right kind of open-ended questions to use in the 90 minutes. You as a leader must know well the materials to be discussed. You choose questions that tap understanding and appreciation. You don't study the materials so you can answer questions about them, but rather so you can ask the most provocative seminar questions to stimulate the dialogue. You want open-ended questions that don't have an exact answer. You want to unlock different interpretations, rather than get all to agree. In the seminar, the goal is not consensus but deeper understanding and appreciation. One should leave a seminar with many unanswered questions.

Once I saw Adler conducting a seminar on Hamlet for fifth graders. He started it by asking how many of them believed in ghosts. It was opportune the seminar took place a week before Halloween. After a good discussion on that topic, he asked if they thought the story of Hamlet could be told without the use of the ghost. They had all kinds of good ideas, including some ingenious ones about fiber optics. The discussion was even more lively when he wondered aloud if Hamlet really was fond of Ophelia. Fifth graders, as you know, are quite expert these days in the area of "who loves whom." I saw 30 fifth graders of mixed abilities who had been coached in reading Hamlet take an active part in the seminar discussion for 90 minutes with an 90-year-old philosopher, and their hands were waving in the air signaling more opinions and contributions when time was up. They loved it. Many found out they were smarter than they had thought they were. Better yet, they liked the play. They were just waiting for a situation in which they could share their ideas and opinions with no tests, no grades, no competition, only peers trying to help themselves and others to better understand and appreciate a literary piece that was deserving of such consideration.

Dialogue is the magic word not only for the principal and adult stakeholders, it is the missing ingredient in all of schooling. With parents, it will open up communication between them and the school. The students will learn from each other, from the teachers, and from every potential source of learning, only if they are helped to develop skill in dialogue. Adult stakeholders who get involved in seminar work will be the best examples of the benefits to be gained from this freeing process. With flexible scheduling, seminar involvement can become a major player in teaching and learning.

SUMMATION

Robert M. Hutchins, in his classic, *The Great Conversation*, tells us that dialogue is the spirit of Western Civilization. Ours is a civilization of dialogue. This dialogue is characterized by the spirit of inquiry in which nothing is left unexamined. I leave it to you to answer these questions: "Has the West lost some of this spirit of inquiry? If it has, is it because we are losing the ability to dialogue"? We no longer are educating our citizens to the point where they can examine propositions and arrive at their own conclusions. Instead, they listen to TV pundits and accept their flimsy opinions, like a group of "ditto heads." The spirit of advocacy has out shouted the spirit of inquiry.

In the next chapter I will be developing a radical notion of teaching and I will try to prove that this original meaning—to show someone how to do something—is essential to developing a Learning Organization. I will introduce the discipline of Systems Thinking when treating of Domain #8, Instruction, and the Learning Environment, but will develop it more fully in the last chapter when we take up Domain #9, Curriculum Design.

The principals I know feel that the most important delegation they make is the mandate to all their staff members to teach the students well. The principals wish they could have an excellent teacher and assistant teacher in each classroom, in the gym, media room, cafeteria, in the office, on the play grounds, on the buses, everywhere. If the teaching goes well, all else goes well. If the teaching goes poorly, nothing else can make up for it. In the next chapter I will discuss "teaching" from the perspective of the principals who are trying to make sure that the delegated instructional responsibilities are carried out in the most effective manner by all the stakeholders.

Teachers and students must always remain free to inquire, to study to evaluate, to gain new maturity and understanding: otherwise our civilization will stagnate and die.
Earl Warren,
Chief Justice of the U.S. Supreme Court

QUESTIONS FOR REFLECTION

1. Why is Delegation such an important skill for principals today? How is it different than it was 20 years ago?

2. What are some of the characteristics shared by principals who are successful delegators? Are there others you could add? What do these characteristics have in common?

3. How can principals delegate important tasks if they don't have a sufficient number of stakeholders with the task relevant maturity needed to carry out the responsibilities?

4. Did the principal who named Abrams, Curry, D'Andrea, and Giggins to the Graduation Committee do a good job? How could she have improved her delegation?

5. Principal Frank Hughes asked a profound question: "How can I get more of the stakeholders to buy into the Shared Vision and pursue the discipline of Personal Mastery?" How did he do it?

6. What does it mean when we say, stakeholders are practicing the discipline of Personal Mastery?

7. What part did the Weekend Workshop at the University play in getting the stakeholders to buy into the Shared Vision? Are there other ways this can be accomplished?

8. Show how Team Learning, Mental Models, Personal Mastery, and Shared Vision depend on the willingness of a group to enter into serious dialogue. How do dialogue and discussion differ?

9. Global Education School became a rallying point for the stakeholders in Frank Hughes' school. Try to think of an overarching theme which could help the stakeholders in your school buy into a Shared Vision. The members of a Learning Organization are always aware of where they are going and how they are going to get there. Does the overarching theme help? How?

10. How could the proficient use of seminars help the stakeholders to become Team Learners? Can the frequent use of seminars rekindle our "spirit of inquiry?" Is it time well spent? Why?

9

TEACHING MEANS SHOWING SOMEONE HOW TO DO SOMETHING

Good schools produce students who love to read and know what is worth reading.

Superintendent Nan Hohlman was born August 3, 1956. Although she didn't realize it for many years, she was born in the peak year of the Baby Boom period. She was 12 years old in 1968, the watershed year in this country. In that year, we lost our innocence as a people and became more cynical, like our ancestors from Europe. Many of us began to have serious doubts about the integrity of our government and its leaders. Youths were cautioning their peers not to trust anyone over 30. Jack Kennedy had been assassinated 5 years earlier, and Camelot came to a crashing end. In 1968, we suffered through the assassinations of Martin Luther King, Jr., and Robert Kennedy. There were weekly bomb scares in college buildings. The Vietnam War was, for many, the smoking gun. However, it was much bigger than that. Americans began to mistrust all institutions. The country went into a spin in 1968, and the gyroscopes aren't working properly to this day. For over 25 years, our ordinary way of doing business has been disrupted.

Nan at 12 knew what was happening. When she entered her teen years it was a different world. Like many principals, she received her early value development prior to 1968, and now is in a position in which she must deal with many students and parents who had their values shaped in the post-1968 culture of rebellion. Two different worlds are competing for ascendance and neither will carry the day. We can't go back to the "good old days" of "Leave it to Beaver," and the values of the '70s and '80s just haven't given us the foundation we need. America is coming out of its adolescence and deciding what kind of an adult it will choose to be. Leaders like Nan will have much to say about schools, and that will make a big difference in the road our country takes.

Nan followed in her mother's footsteps and became a teacher. A good student, she went through college painlessly, not even challenged in graduate school. I often wondered what made her so special. At 38 she is the youngest superintendent in the Southeast. She sometimes wonders if she went too far too fast. In one sense, she had no choice. She stood out so spectacularly, and possessed such gifts of mind and heart, it was inevitable that she would be wooed by administrators to accept more and more responsibility.

Nan was chosen state Teacher of the Year when she was 26. She was named principal of a middle school at 31. Now, 8 years later, she has had a year's experience running a small, very poor, racially mixed, rural school system which is on a state list of school systems at risk. Some 12 school systems are doing so poorly on the end-of-course tests, there is a threat the state will take them over if there isn't a great improvement. Nan and her schools are under real stress. From all reports, she is doing her best to bring these schools up to standards. In this chapter, Nan and I will be sharing with you ideas we discussed on the role of the principal as the Instructional Leader.

Trying to understand Nan's phenomenal professional success, I was able to pick out three things that contributed heavily. First, her mother had been a successful elementary school teacher and always talked about her teaching years with great joy and excitement. Second, Nan's father was a reporter at, and later editor of, a very small newspaper. He was an avid reader, interested in a wide range of subjects. Nan says he was a newspaperman by day and a classical scholar by night. Both parents valued learning above all else. They read aloud to each other nightly. Hearing them gave Nan a longing to be old enough to join in the fun. The third, and perhaps the most important, contributing factor to Nan's rise to fame was a mixed blessing. When Nan was 12 years old her mother, in her 40s, had a boy baby, christened Mark, who had Down syndrome. This changed the whole family configuration. Nan took over the teaching of her newborn brother. This pushed her to grow up almost overnight. She reveled in every minute spent introducing Mark to her world of play and study. Mark within his limitations was a good learner. With infinite patience Nan helped him climb the developmental steps with surprising ease. Nan was that rare person who seemed to know how to teach without ever having had training. That isn't quite true. Her mother and father had been excellent teachers during Nan's first 12 years. Nan tells me, "We tend to teach the way we were taught and I was well-taught." As she continued the task of teaching Mark, their relationship flourished. He followed her around constantly and waited impatiently for her to come home from school to teach him how to do new things. His constant question was, "Nan, any new things to teach me?"

I was surprised that Nan didn't choose special education in college. When I asked her why, she said she thought all children should be taught the way exceptional children are taught. Working with her brother Mark, she never compared his achievements with those of any other child. She helped him compete with himself, to improve his performance to his own level of satisfaction. Nan also used the family movie camera to record the learning experiences of her brother. Nan laughingly says, "I was building a portfolio for him and didn't know I was doing it." Mark loved to watch the home movies over and over again. He cheered when he saw himself learning to walk, talk, write, draw, and swim. By the time he was 10 years old, Mark was the family projectionist. At 24, Mark is gainfully employed and uses a camcorder as part of his work.

THE PRINCIPAL AS INSTRUCTIONAL LEADER

When I wanted to develop ideas on how a principal can exert his or her influence in the school to improve the quality of instruction, I happened to be working with Nan in New York City during a 6-week summer course. This gave us the opportunity to work cooperatively on this question of helping principals delegate instructional responsibilities while doing everything possible to ensure that the quality of instruction was not only maintained, but enhanced. This is an area in which Nan had real success when she was a principal. Now, as a superintendent, she is searching for ways to help her principals enhance delegated instructional skills and empower their teachers. She wants her principals to give highest priority to developing their teachers into Team Learners and students of teaching.

We read three documents: First, the chapter on Instruction, Domain #8, from *Principals For Our Changing Schools*. Second, we read a wonderful book, *A Letter To Teachers*, by Vito Perrone. Third, I shared with Nan a copy of an unpublished manuscript, *Show How: An Inquiry Into The Art Of Teaching*, by Gabriel Moran, a book on the philosophical understanding of "to teach." With these three exceptional source documents and our own experience both in teaching and working with teachers, we set out to discuss the topic of the principals' delegating teaching responsibilities in their schools.

DOMAIN 8—INSTRUCTION AND THE LEARNING ENVIRONMENT

Although Moran is of the opinion that definitions should be held back until we have discussed a word or topic for some time, accepting the ambiguities involved in the many different meanings attached to it, we thought it was better to set forth the excellent definition Fenwick W. English and his associates offered in *Principals For Our Changing Schools* (16):

"Instruction and the Learning Environment Creating a school culture for learning; envisioning and enabling with others instructional auxiliary programs for the improvement of teaching and learning; recognizing the developmental needs of students; ensuring appropriate instructional methods; designing positive learning experiences; accommodating differences in cognition and achievement; mobilizing the participation of appropriate people or groups to develop these programs and to establish a positive learning environment."

Nan remarked she wished she had had that definition when she was a principal. It challenges principals to serve as instructional leaders in four different ways: they possess the basic knowledge about teaching and learning; they plan the instructional programs with the teachers; they do all they can to empower teachers in implementing their instructional plans; and, finally, they evaluate the quality of instruction in the school.

Of the four ways a principal works to improve the quality of instruction, the one we were most interested in was the first. What formative knowledge does a principal need to be able to function as an instructional leader? Principals must know school curricular trends which will be discussed in the next chapter. Principals need to know new approaches to organizing schools. It is in this task that we hope the model of a Learning Organization will help. Perhaps most crucial is their grasp of state of the art instructional media and methodology. Finally, they need wide knowledge of the research on improving student outcomes. In this chapter, I will cover some of these subjects. It would be helpful first to answer two questions. What do good teachers do and what do they leave out? What does "to teach" really mean?

English and associates tell us that effective principals perceive instructional leadership as a collegial process. "Effective principals:

◆ hold teachers and students responsible to high expectations;
◆ spend a major portion of their day working with teachers to improve the educational program;

- ◆ work to identify and diagnose instructional problems; and
- ◆ become deeply involved in school culture and
  climate to influence student learning in positive
  ways." (17)

We agreed that holding both the teachers and the students
to high expectations is probably the most important thing the
principal does for instructional quality. Nan says parents often
complain when the principal holds the teachers and students to
high expectations. Some parents actually say they don't want
their children to have homework because it takes time away
from the family activities. I found this hard to believe, but
having heard it so often, I know it must be true. I wondered if
there was anything a principal could do to get parents to see
how important these high expectations are to the successful
education of their children? Nan thinks that some parents are
suspicious of the whole educational enterprise. In her new job
as superintendent, she is spending much time in community
outreach trying to get parents to meet in small groups at the
mills and factories where they work. She is trying to make
them active stakeholders in their childrens' schooling. After 1
year, she now has five firms which allow her and other school
personnel to come to the plants and meet for an hour and a
half lunch period with parents. The parents get a free lunch
and an extra hour off from work to attend meetings.

She tries to convince parents that the jobs they hold are
vanishing, and there will be no similar jobs for their children.
Unless their children get better educated they won't find work
at home and will have to move out of the county. Better
educated young people will move into the area and take the
technical jobs. The next step is to try to convince parents and
employers that we are already deeply into a global economy.
Their children will be competing for jobs not just against kids
from Ohio but from Turkey, South Korea, and Bangladesh.
They need better schooling and another language.

The parents are beginning to listen, but the biggest change
Nan notices is the more positive attitude of the CEOs of these
mills and factories. In the past, they seemed willing to hire
anyone regardless of whether or not they graduated or

performed well in high school. The bosses didn't have to worry about those things because the jobs were "dumbed down" so much anyone could fill them. Now, as the mills become more technically sophisticated, the workers have to be able to read, speak, think, write, listen, and calculate. Computers are becoming a part of every machine and instrument in the shop; an employee has to become computer literate to survive. The CEOs of mills are beginning to realize they have to take more responsibility for improving the level of schooling for their present and future workers. It isn't just altruism, it's a matter of survival. Nan is reaping some of this good harvest. The mill and factory owners are beginning to cooperate in many ways with the schools.

Nan doesn't come from North Carolina, and was most envious when I told her that the General Assembly in North Carolina has just passed a law which mandates that companies give employees time off to attend school meetings and volunteer. This state law, modelled after one in Virginia, requires businesses to grant employees 4 hours of leave every year so they can visit their children's school or participate in mentoring or tutoring programs. Also, North Carolina State employees get 8 hours of paid school leave per year for school work. Compared with other efforts designed to improve the curricula and rewrite standardized tests, the school leave program is relatively simple. However, some of our top educators think it might reap even greater rewards. Nan agrees: "When you get active parental involvement, you see exciting things happen. There is no better way to raise the academic expectations for teachers and students than to get the parents convinced that their whole way of life depends on better educational outcomes for their children."

Remember, Nan is now running a school system in the Appalachian Southeast in which less than 50% graduate from high school. She tells me that 80 to 85% of the people in her district like things just the way they are. They are satisfied with the schools just the way they are, in spite of the fact that the school system has been put on probation. Nan knows the locals come from a culture that does not put a whole lot of stock in people sitting around desks, thinking and talking and doing research and reading. They often say they live in the best little county in the whole U.S.A. They can hunt and fish when they want. They don't have ulcers like big city people. They aren't afraid to walk the roads at night. They have a strong sense of community and pride themselves on their ability to take care of each other. They know they are paid about 80% of what they could earn in other states. They even know their schools aren't as good as some up North, but who cares—their kids don't need to go to college, they can work in the mill. They have 1,001 stories about highly educated management types who fall over their own feet on the mill floor and don't have the common sense of a mule.

Nan tells me it reminds her of a short story by Robert Louis Stevenson, about people who lived on the rim of a volcano which was going to erupt real soon. The people paid no attention to the scientists who were trying to warn them to take precautions and advised them to move down the mountain away from the paths the lava would flow. That could have saved them but they didn't believe the volcano would erupt. It hadn't in the memory of the oldest men. Nan is not discouraged. She feels with the help of the mill owners whose self-interest dictates that they cooperate in raising academic expectations in the schools, with the help of laws like the ones passed in Virginia and North Carolina, the educators will be able to slowly, but surely, get the parents to realize how important better schooling is for their children.

As we talked in New York City about raising academic expectations for teachers and students, we realized that the problem was not confined to the South. For a million school students in New York City the goal was exactly the same. How to get the parents to cooperate with the schools in encouraging their students to study harder and learn more? How to get the teachers to really believe that the students sitting in front of them had much higher potential than most people realized? How to get the students to aim higher? We were sitting less than 3 miles from Central Park East Secondary School, an innercity high school that has become a beacon for struggling schools across the country. The statement of purpose for CPESS is worth quoting. It is called the Promise.

"At CPESS we make an important promise to every student—one we know we can keep. We promise our students that when they graduate from CPESS, they will have learned to use their minds—and to use their minds well.

In every class, in every subject, students will learn to ask and to answer these questions:

♦ From whose viewpoint are we seeing or reading or hearing? From what angle or perspective?

♦ How do we know what we know? What is the evidence, and how reliable is it?

♦ How are things, events, or people connected to each other? What is the cause and what is the effect? How do they "fit" together?

♦ So what? Why does it matter? What does it all mean? Who cares?

We are committed to the idea that a diploma is a meaningful piece of paper, not one that says only that the student has "stuck it out" through high school. A CPESS diploma tells the student—and the world—that the student has not only mastered specific fields of study but is curious and thoughtful, above all, has learned 'how to learn' and to use his/her learning to deal with new issues and problems." (Central Park East Secondary School, 1988)

We didn't get a chance to visit CPESS but we visited other New York City schools very much like it that were doing the very things which can and should be done in schools across the country. Nan and her planning group are using the Promise from CPESS as a model of the kinds of higher expectations they want for their students.

Moving on, we agreed that principals who want the best quality instruction in their schools must spend a major portion of their working day helping to improve the educational program. Nan has found that principals who use lead teachers in a Peer Coaching Program are finding good results. The better teachers are given time to coach teachers who request help, both in their classrooms and in small groups dedicated to learning better teaching skills. Many teachers seem less threatened working directly with their peers rather than the principal.

Nan believes that principals can use time saved through Peer Coaching to help teachers identify and diagnose instructional problems, and become more deeply involved in school culture. Nan is convinced that the school culture is a powerful force for influencing student learning in a positive way. Nan and I agree, from our observations, that effective principals organize their day so that their time and attention are focused on instructional rather than routine matters. Less effective principals use their time poorly, letting trivial things dominate. They should be explaining Learning Styles to the teachers. They should be challenging the teachers who spend 80% of their classroom time in didactic teaching with little time devoted for coaching and none for seminars. Instead, they are strict in maintaining the traditional classroom organization that promotes uniformity. They praise teachers who enforce rigid control whether the students are learning or not. They are leery of flexible scheduling, team teaching, cooperative learning, and any departures from the regular routine.

Nan claims that her better principals have the knack of changing the school facilities to make instructional innovations possible. A clever principal can take an old school of the "egg crate" variety and modify it so that it accommodates different groupings and teacher modalities. Given a chance to design a school building, he or she knows just what is needed. They work from a profile of children not from some theory of education. They all seem to agree that the school should allow for more hands-on experience, more small group activities, more fluidity of movement. Some principals agree with Howard Gardner that school buildings should be more like childrens' museums than like old factory model schools with fixed seating.

In Domain #8, English and his associates offer 22 performance standards that a principal should meet if he or she is to be skilled in delegating instructional duties and ensuring that the quality of instruction in the school is maintained and enhanced. I recommend that you study all of them, but in discussing the material with Nan she and I agreed that a dozen of them should be highlighted.To do a good job as instructional leader a principal should be able to:

1. identify the key attributes of skilled instructional leaders;
2. be in touch with the major sources and findings of research on instruction;
3. describe the implications of learning style for instructional design;
4. describe the major forms of school scheduling and organizational structures and their relationship to programmatic effects and potential learner outcomes;
5. identify several current teaching models;
6. discuss a variety of supervisory techniques and describe their application to teachers;
7. identify several elements of school culture that support teaching and learning;
8. outline a change process to improve student outcomes;
9. analyze relationships between school plant and instructional programs and suggest steps to modify a traditional facility to improve the learning environment and faculty collegiality;
10. apply critical pedagogy to three disparate socio-economic settings;
11. describe several staffing patterns and their relationship to various instructional practices; and
12. design a budget process with staff that reflects school priorities for the instructional program.

A LETTER TO TEACHERS

The second book Nan and I discussed is entitled *A Letter To Teachers,* written by Vito Perrone. This is a must for all principals in spite of the fact that it is addressed to teachers. Any principal who places a high priority on instructional improvement will find this book a treasure chest of good ideas. Imagine that you are communicating with the teachers in your school and take some of Perrone's ideas and see how relevant they could be.

Perrone tells teachers they should engage in serious discussions about the large purposes of schooling. These are the guiding principles that inform teachers' practices, curriculum patterns, organizational structures, and relationships with students and their parents. These purposes should be more fully in our consciousness as we plan instructional programs. When large purposes lose their central position in the minds of principals and teachers, these schools tend to drift. They lose their independence and their educational and social power. Remember Frank Hughes whose stakeholders at a weekend workshop discussed their large purposes and were able to develop the vision for a Global Education School? Creating this vision offered a new direction for the school and energized the stakeholders. The Learning Organization which evolved is still pulsing with large purposes. That is why it is so alive and exciting.

According to Perrone education at its best is a moral and intellectual endeavor always beginning with children and young people and their intentions and needs. A drifting school has lost sight of the students, their intentions and their needs, and is focused on less important issues.

Whether the students learn the mechanics of reading and writing is less important than whether they learn to love reading and writing. My wife writes over 200 Christmas cards each year. Every card contains a long personal message. During the year she writes several hundred cards and letters. She writes well and enjoys writing. She loves people and finds this a wonderful way to keep in touch with them throughout the year. Her teacher was her beloved father who wrote to people in the same way. He didn't encourage her to do it, but seeing him enjoying it and making so many people happy, she just picked it up as her hobby. Now he didn't teach her the mechanics of writing. Some teachers in elementary school helped her develop that skill. She finds great satisfaction in using her writing skills. Her facility in writing gives her pleasure and brings joy to hundreds of others. How few people there are today who find it enjoyable to write.

Nan and I talked for a long time about teachers who have that great gift of helping students not only to read, write, speak, listen, and think, but somehow make it fun. The students who leave a teacher at the end of the year with a love for reading will be able to educate themselves for the rest of their lives and have a great time doing it. This is the standard of instruction principals seek.

Often teachers are more concerned that students hear about knowledge—that is, sit in places where knowledge is dispensed rather than have the experience of personally constructing knowledge. Sometimes we stress the importance of competition over affording them the experience of real cooperative learning. Sometimes teachers seem to imply that the world is simple and neatly ordered like the text books, instead of complex and uncertain. Too often teachers stress the importance of students accepting the authority that exists around them in the classroom structure and in the text books, rather than helping them learn how to challenge that authority. Some of my teachers must have taught me that it was acceptable to bring a healthy skepticism to the world. Nan says her mother and father both encouraged their children to think independently.

WHAT A GOOD TEACHER LOOKS LIKE

The large purposes are what motivate the good teachers to do the things they do in and out of the classroom. These purposes determine the relations between the good teachers and their students. There are basic things that good teachers do to improve instruction.

Good teachers focus first on the students and are very attentive to who they are. They ride the bus now and again to see where they come from. They learn their cultural backgrounds, their strengths, the kinds of learning that motivates them. They learn what kinds of questions turn them on.

Good teachers know that bare walls are teachers but walls covered with interesting and colorful materials are better teachers. Good teachers seem to know that there are other teachers all around the classroom—the gold fish, the cactus plant, the globe, the flags, pictures, the custodian blowing leaves outside the window. Good teachers know that the quality of the students' learning is the real measure of a school. They are more interested in the quality of learning than in the quantity of information ingested and regurgitated. These good teachers are swimming upstream because the end of term tests measure the quantity of learning rather than the quality. Only life measures the quality of schooling, and the results come in many years after the students have left school. Nan and I jokingly said it would be better to pick the teacher of the year later, when the students were 35, and thinking back on which teachers cared about the quality of their learning and taught with that purpose.

Good teachers try to use fresh materials instead of second-hand commercial stuff. The use of text books written for a mass audience has killed our natural curiosity about subjects. I knew a principal who directed a private school on City Island, a section of the Bronx. This little island in New York harbor has a limited population and many of the families have lived there for generations. The teachers and students made a historical study of the island. They were especially interested in the ancestors of the students. They went to the cemetery to garner as many family names as they could. The students went to City Hall to copy documents which revealed the ages, marital status, number of children, gender, occupation, cause of death, etc. They went to the churches to get more information. They went to Ellis Island to see the names of many of their ancestors who had entered the country from that port.

Nan was fascinated as I explained how all the teachers, regardless of what subjects they taught, had their students using copies of original documents which had personal significance. The math teacher used butcher and baker bills to compare them with today's supermarket prices. Then she compared the wages a laborer earned in 1843 with those earned in 1943 and 1993. They were able to find local histories, diaries, business records, health records, and old newspaper articles which helped fill in the missing pieces. They collaborated on a book, much to the delight of all City Island residents. This is what good teachers do. They get involved with students in doing something which has real significance to both.

An added benefit was that the City Island teachers did this research collaboratively. No one teacher could do it alone. Good teachers engage other teachers in the constant search for new and fresh material. The state and federal governments churn out excellent research materials which can be tailored to fit the needs of school children. The *National Geographic* is a gold mine. A recent special issue on water would make an excellent overarching topic to bring all the teachers and students together for a year applying this fresh information to problems in their own localities. Instead of taking the children only to the fire house and the police station, what about the Water Treatment Plant?

Good teachers are noted for taking their students seriously, but not themselves. They spend a lot of time getting to know their students. They try to know their interests, their preferred learning styles, the meaning of their gestures and facial expressions, their ways of approaching new materials, their general outlook on the world, their frustration level, how they take success and failure, their preferences in food, sports, clothes, music, companions, hobbies, sports teams, etc. Some good teachers I know work at it very systematically. They have 3" by 5" cards with the students' pictures attached so they can become familiar with them in the first couple of weeks. On the card they jot down new information which will help them as teachers to keep up with the changing lives of their students.

Also, how many teachers allow the students to get close enough to them so they can really say they know the teacher? Nan tells a story about one of her teachers with the improbable name of Elias Turnipseed. He is called "Corny" Turnipseed by one and all. Corny farms a small, 20 acre tract when he isn't teaching science in the local high school. He specializes in the study of corn. When he isn't teaching or tending the farm he is studying corn. Corny has research published in the best journals. His classroom is a genuine corn museum. All the kids look for new corn-connected things with the hope that Corny will include them in the corn museum. He always attaches a label to each item which credits the donor. This is a surefire way to fame in the small town. Corny knows all the types and subtypes of corn and has been able to create some mixed varieties which are used commercially. He knows about the skill of the Native Americans who developed the growing of corn into a science. During his vacation, he drove his family to

Massachusetts to visit the corn Hall of Fame at the University of Massachusetts and to meet an agriculture prof there who knew more about corn than he did.

At harvest time Corny invites all his current students and their parents to a picnic on his farm. It is one of the town's big social events. At the picnic, corn is served in over 57 varieties: roasted, boiled, baked, corn bread, corn syrup, corn cakes, corn relish, and, finally, popcorn. Fried chicken (corn fed of course) is grudgingly served for those who are not avid corn connoisseurs.

This high school science teacher over the last 12 years has produced 24 students, who went on to earn graduate degrees in the field of agriculture. They are all working in corn research. Nan says Corny has been selected teacher of the year so often he has disqualified himself. He can't wait until one of his students gets that honor.

It isn't just the 24 students who went on to college to study agriculture who profited from Corny's passion for corn. All his students seem to understand and appreciate science and the scientific method. They have studied with a master teacher who is passionate about something, and they watch him learning more about his area of expertise daily. All students have acted as lab or field assistants. They have had "hands-on experience" with corn, the one food that could feed every American and still leave enough to sell millions of bushels to the world.

Nan knows how fortunate she is to have a teacher like Elias Turnipseed. She is trying to get her principals to encourage teachers to organize their classwork around the area of their passion. A third grade teacher is the daughter of a watch and clock maker. Her passion is clocks of all kinds. She didn't see any reason to bring her hobby into her classes. Nan convinced her that all we know from the great human conversation can be integrated around the concept "time" and our efforts to measure it with timepieces. Nan and she are trying to figure how to get third graders interested in sun dials, water clocks, sand clocks, wind-up clocks with springs, and the new watches run by tiny batteries. The whole third grade curriculum could be taught with clocks as the integrating concept. Just as corn is a staple of everyday living so is time. *A teacher with a passion for learning anything can teach almost anyone to want to learn something.*

TO CHANGE SCHOOLS INTO LEARNING ORGANIZATIONS WE HAVE TO REFLECT ON THE MORAL DIMENSION OF TEACHING

One of the most striking things about education today is the way professional educators shy away from using the phrase "to teach." Some writers have gone to the extent of refusing to use the word "teach," preferring to use only the word "learn." According to Gabriel Moran, the author of *Show How: The Art Of Teaching,* the reason for this reluctance to write about teaching or even use the word in discussion is a serious one. Teaching is a moral activity and this scares many people in our secular age. I think much school reform awaits our confronting this anomaly. Even when teaching is mentioned, it is spoken of in a restrictive manner. It is assumed that all teaching is classroom teaching. People have an ethical and moral problem about classroom teaching. By what right does this teacher impose her values on my son? Who gave this public school teacher the right to tell my daughter how to live her life?

Nan confronts this problem daily. She knows that schools should be teaching the best of our society's cultural legacy and this includes virtues to be admired. "We can't absolve the schools from all responsibility," she says. But she makes it clear that some parents don't want the school to mention God or angels. One of her teachers has just discovered a new movement called Character Counts, founded by the Josephson Institute of Ethics. Nan insisted that I mention it in the book. I dutifully copied this presentation from Character Counts:

- ◆ Express your concern to all individuals and organizations that influence youth.
- ◆ Teach your family the importance of character by living according to the six ethical values. (Trustworthiness, Respect, Responsibility, Fairness, Caring, and Citizenship)
- ◆ Hold yourself and others more strictly accountable to live up to the six core ethical values.

◆ Inform yourself about what is going on in the
  schools and other youth organizations.

◆ Create an atmosphere of positive and negative
  consequences that encourages and prizes good
  character.

◆ Support individuals and organizations engaged in
  character development activities.

Nan is working with the teacher who discovered Character
Counts to form a group of stakeholders to design a plan for
implementing this type of character education in the curriculum. I warned her that she would probably get sued real
soon by a Kindergarten student who, in conscience, cannot
accept the value of caring. More important, Nan has done what
few superintendents have been able to do. She convinced her
State Board of Education that the whole idea of putting a school
system on probation was counterproductive. They gave her 5
years to implement a plan in which her school system doesn't
compete with any other school system in the state. It competes
with itself. Nan has promised that with more support from the
State Department of Education her school system in 5 years will
make a 50% improvement against its last year's results on the
statewide test. Nan was jubilant. Many of her teachers are
hopeful, starting to teach the students not the subjects, or for
the sake of the tests. Nan is still wrestling with the morality of
teaching, and so am I. She has already shown real character.

Moran teaches that in the 20th century, the phrase "moral
education" came to mean a specialized area; not the opposite
of immoral, but of neutral amoral education. A special set of
techniques was developed for moral education through moral
development. Incidentally, educators who specialize in moral
education are very suspicious of "teaching." They say the
teacher should never say that something is right or wrong.

Instead of butting heads with others, the moral educators
tend to move in the direction of moral development. With this
process, children just become more moral with the passage of
time. Since they develop morally anyway, we don't really need
"teaching." Time will take care of everything. Piaget's influential work on moral judgment (later expanded by Lawrence

Kohlberg) was critical of adult interference in the development of the child's moral judgment. He was very harsh on school teachers, believing that their attempts to teach morals are detrimental. My experience over the last 45 years with juvenile delinquents in training schools and adult prisoners in maximum security prisons, flies in the face of that assertion. In my experience, people don't just grow more moral with the passage of time. Some get a lot worse.

What a pickle we find ourselves in! We think moral development is important. Public school teachers aren't supposed to get involved because of the law of separation of church and state. The moral educators believe the process is more or less automatic and, therefore, we don't need to have teachers meddling in this process. What about those homes in which the moral modeling is either nonexistent (parents aren't around) or is totally negative or in conflict? Will those children be subjected to teaching on morals? The teachers who avoid the subject are implicitly saying moral education is not important. Finally, some parents don't speak about moral values in front of the children or, when they do, their disagreements cancel each other out. What moral teachers will influence the children? They will have teaching from TV, radio, tapes, CDs, movies, video games, peers, rappers, rockers, sports, dances, advertisements, government, celebrities, and fast food restaurants. The moral influence of the family, church, and neighborhood have been diminishing since 1968. Most teachers are not school teachers. The TV may be the most influential teacher of young children in this country and we educators aren't teaching the students how to watch TV with a critical mind. A first step in moral education is critical thinking.

Public Broadcasting Services is about to launch what may be one of their greatest educational ventures. It is introducing a new lineup designed in part to wean kids from TV addiction. Called "The Ready to Learn Service," it will offer 9 hours of daily children's shows that are meant to get children and their parents involved in activities beyond the tube. The goal is to prepare preschool children for kindergarten through shows that teach not only language fundamentals, but also skills such as negotiation, experimentation, and finishing school-related tasks. PBS promises to send out support materials that will help adults use the TV as a learning tool, "to get them reading, singing, turning the TV off, and spending time with the children." We know that the 19 million preschoolers in the U.S. watch 15 billion hours of TV each year. TV can be a good teacher which stretches the child's mind instead of stuffing it with violent images. Nan and I wish PBS all success. We realize there is no turning back. TV is a permanent fixture in American family life. It is a powerful teacher. Now we have a chance to make it a valued teacher rather than one that corrupts youngsters by pandering to their worst instincts.

TO TEACH MEANS AND HAS ALWAYS MEANT TO SHOW SOMEONE HOW TO DO SOMETHING

Moran says, "The moral dilemma, which is inherent in all human attempts to teach, has been exacerbated by the collapse of all teaching into one form." Rousseau tells the teacher to remember he is strong and the child is weak. If a reasonable explanation doesn't suffice to get him to do what he should, then the tutor can use sheer power to control the situation. How often have principals heard a teacher screaming at a recalcitrant student, "This is going on your permanent record in the principal's office." Here is the moral problem: teaching always has been and always will be situated in a power relation. Only two areas of teaching are exempt: teaching adults and teaching moral education. Even some adult teaching smacks of a power relationship when the training is carried on in a company, and the director of training grades the trainees on willingness to learn, cooperation, etc. Most moral education to date refuses to take a stand.

For over a thousand years "to teach" has meant to show someone how to do something. In the most basic sense, this "showing how" starts with bodily gestures that invite a bodily response. A great example of teaching is the way a father teaches his son to swim. He doesn't show him pictures of a child swimming. He goes into the pool with him. I watch this many times a week in the pool I use for my daily swim. The father is in the pool, and he puts his hand under the youngster's stomach to hold him up. Then he takes one arm and pulls it through the motion of an overhand stroke. Next he takes the other arm and does the same. Now the parent places the youngster on the side of the pool and demonstrates the arm movement in the water. First the right arm goes over and under, then the left arm follows suit. They then go back into the water and repeat the procedure. I won't bore you with the full lesson, but I want to make the point. The prime example of teaching is showing someone how to do something physical. Think of the time you taught your daughter to ride a two-wheel bicycle. *As long as the teaching is close to bodily gestures and bodily response, the moral issue is easy to handle.* The teacher is showing the youngster how to perform a skill. The only justification needed is the expertise of the teacher. He knows how to swim himself and feels comfortable teaching his son how to swim. The son wants to learn. He is not being coerced. No moral problem here.

The only way we can know that teaching took place is that the son picks up the arm movements and is able to perform them the following week. The only proof that teaching exists is the existence of learning. There is learning now which wasn't before. If after 10 lessons the boy doesn't make any progress in the water, the father can't go home and say to his wife, "I taught Gilbert how to swim but he didn't learn." Truth is, if he didn't learn, the father didn't teach. I can't emphasize this distinction enough. Schools won't reform until teachers begin to realize that going through the motions of teaching by standing in front of a class and speaking loudly or reading from a text book for 45 minutes is not necessarily teaching. It is definitely emoting. It isn't lecturing, because lecturing is a form of teaching.

How can we explain why the student does not learn what the teacher teaches? The answer lies in the recognition that the student is always facing many teachers. The child learns what has been taught by one or more teachers, but it may not be the lesson that the school teacher is trying to teach. *Once we acknowledge that all children are learning something at all times, then we have made a giant breakthrough in finding many different ways of reaching children.* If we know that the pictures on the classroom wall, the mobile hanging from the ceiling, the goldfish in the bowl, the two students physically close to him, the trucks moving dirt just outside the window, are all teachers, we then have increased our opportunities for reaching more students and guiding their mental and moral growth. Not only is the child learning every minute, he is being taught by a multitude of teachers every minute of his waking life. Any person, place, or thing that shows someone how to do something is a teacher. For me, the ocean is one of my most powerful teachers. She teaches me respect, awe, appreciation, fear, delight, time, space, perspective, reverence, patience, etc. Gabriel Moran says, "The ultimate subject of 'to show someone how to do something' is the universe of living and nonliving things." The world is filled with teachers.

It would be a shame if we left out one of Moran's best points. He tells us that animals have much to teach us. Children seem to know instinctively that animals are great teachers. Some adults forget many animal species have survived a lot longer than we humans have. In the process, they have amassed a great store of survival experience. They can show us how to live and how to die. We are the only animals who foresee our death, but we seem to forget it and live as if we were immortal, and our bodies could be endlessly repaired with cannibalized donor parts. Animals learn but they also teach, training their young to do the essential things for self-preservation and survival of the species. Some of the lessons animals could teach us would be the place of ritual in interspecies conflict.

Another thing we can learn from the animals is that we are animals ourselves. Whatever humans try to teach, in a specifically human fashion, they can never get away from their animal nature. Watch lions in the unnatural surroundings of their caged existence, and see how they walk back and forth endlessly, and constantly stretch to keep their muscles strong and loose. Watch 30 youngsters in the unnatural surrounding of a fifth grade classroom sitting and fidgeting. Young animals crave movement and changing scenery. In Japanese and German schools much more time is devoted to physical activities, and not just at recess. The three legs of teaching include bodily activity (doing something), silence (being someone), and, finally, words (saying or hearing something). We tend to overplay the last in our teaching. Silence and bodily activity may be more effective at times. Humans do too much talking and explaining. Animals just practice and teach their young to practice activities that are life-preserving. The mature cat washes the body of the kitten and slowly the kitten takes over and washes itself. Moran tells us that mother cats know the best time to clean a kitten is while it is eating. Throughout its life, the cat will associate eating with cleaning. Animals teach life, health, and safety tips to their offspring. Everyday in the U.S. 13 children die and another 30 are injured from gunfire. Why don't we teach health and safety?

Our next mistake is underplaying the teaching role of parents. As long as we talk about teachers and restrict the definition to school teachers, we are making a giant mistake. School teachers are only a small auxiliary force meant to facilitate certain types of academic learning. The parent is responsible for all teaching that goes on with their children. The school teacher is a trained specialist who knows how to teach certain learning skills and to open veins of knowledge for exploration, discovery, and understanding. The parent delegates the responsibility of teaching these skills to the teacher, never giving up his or her responsibility even for the academic education of the offspring. How far is that from the realistic situation in our day, when many parents literally dump their children on the school, and blithely expect the school to assume full responsibility for all the teaching the child needs.

Nan wanted to talk more about the moral dilemma in teaching. She found it hard to see exactly what Moran was driving at. Certainly there was no moral problem with teachers in the early grades showing students how to print words, how to sound words, how to do the mechanics of writing, of singing, coloring, counting blocks, and figuring simple number combinations. I explained to her that the moral dilemma in the meaning of "to teach" arises when the words are separated from silence and bodily movements. The moral problem comes to a head when teaching is equated with words alone. The moral problem can be stated simply: As the child learns more in school, there are moments when she has to overcome immediate feelings of fear or laziness to master a complex human skill (for example reading comprehension). At this juncture no teacher should simply run roughshod over the immediate feelings of the student. Teaching requires a discovering of the rhythms of the learner's constitution.

One of the best ways to handle the moral dilemma of teaching is the serious study of the learning style of each student and matching the teaching to the learning style. When teachers are aware that teaching rests on three legs—the bodily organism, silence, and words—they will be less obtrusive and insensitive. Unfortunately, in school, teaching with words consumes 80% of the time and only 10% each is left for bodily movements and silence. Afterall, the standardized tests can only measure the words, so teachers tend to neglect the other two important legs. Teaching is moral as long as it uses all three legs and tailors the teaching to the students' needs.

Moran says, "The most effective teachers do not begin by setting out examples, but by being examples." Although teachers aren't allowed to teach religion in public schools, every good teacher I know teaches morals all the time by his or her example. They don't specifically intend to teach these values, but by their example they model them, and the students are free to accept or reject them. There is no coercion. Students don't learn to be virtuous by hearing sermons. If they learn to be virtuous at all, it is because they have the opportunity to associate with virtuous people. Virtue is taught all day long by virtuous members of the community. We should try to pick teachers who are virtuous members of the community. There are many teachers whose classroom teaching offers students the opportunity to be in the presence of virtuous people. These teachers go about their business without reflecting much on their role as models. They do their job and show the youngsters that there are self-disciplined adults who have a sense of humor as well as a sense of honor. Many school children find the classroom a haven of peace, safety, and order as they come from a world of utter chaos.

Nan and I agreed that those teachers who use all the three general types of teaching—Didactic, Coaching, and Seminars—will come closest to running a moral classroom. These teachers seriously study the learning styles of each of their students and blend their teaching with bodily activity, silence, and words. When a teacher takes the time to really understand when, where, by what means, at what time of day, in what form of teaching each student learns best, he or she is modeling virtue and balancing the classroom power. The teacher isn't saying, "I taught the material, it's up to you to learn it." Rather, the teacher has grasped Moran's idea that the only proof that teaching exists is the existence of learning. Then the academic teaching/learning is also moral. Nan and I concluded we have more morally good teachers than most people realize. Principals have the job of making it easier for those thoughtful, generous, and sensitive teachers who vary their teaching styles according to the distinctive learning needs of the students. They teach students not subject matter, and respect the individuality of students along with their need for bodily activity and periods of silence.

SUMMATION

In this chapter, I stressed the role of the principal as the instructional leader. Looking at a profile of a great teacher and reflecting on a rather original meaning of teaching, "showing someone how to do something," should help principals fulfill their respective roles. In the next, and final, chapter we will discuss the role of curriculum in preparing students for continued learning in adult life. There is a real connection between the moral aspects of teaching and the choice of curriculum including the freedom of the teacher to have some input into curriculum development. The principal, who Adler calls the principal teacher, must have skill and knowledge in dealing with the most important topic of curriculum. I will share with you some of the ideas on curriculum from Domain #9 in *Principals For Our Changing Schools*. Additionally, I will discuss some insights from Mortimer Adler, Vito Perrone, and E.D. Hirsch relating to the function of the curriculum in encouraging a life-long love of learning. Some curricula are more moral than others.

QUESTIONS FOR REFLECTION

1. What did Nan Hohlman mean when she said she didn't go into special education because she really believed that all

children should be taught the way exceptional children are taught?

2. Why is it no surprise that effective principals hold teachers and students responsible to high expectations, and spend a major portion of their day working with teachers to improve the educational program? How do they accomplish this?

3. Read over, once again, the "Promise" made by the stakeholders of Central Park East Secondary School. Could it be applied to your school? What changes in instruction would have to be made?

4. Effective principals know what good teachers look like. Make a list of the defining characteristics or attributes of good teachers. How can you help fair teachers become good ones?

5. The story about Elias "Corny" Turnipseed illustrates well this principle: *A teacher with a passion for learning anything can teach almost anyone to want to learn something.* Why don't teachers bring into class and share with students the things that really interest them? What we are trying to teach is a passion for continued learning. How can we do that if we don't model such a passion?

6. The moral problem with teaching comes down to this: teaching always has been and always will be situated in a power relation. How can we avoid misusing our power as school teachers while at the same time taking a stand on moral issues? Solve this dilemma and we will be able to improve.

7. (a) *Once we acknowledge that all children are learning something at all times then we have made a giant breakthrough in finding many different ways of reaching children.* (b) *Great teachers do not begin by setting out examples, but by being examples.* How would we teach differently if we really acknowledged these two truths? Principals can help teachers accept these truths? How?

10

THE CURRICULUM—PREPARING THE YOUNG FOR CONTINUED LEARNING IN THE 21ST CENTURY

It is interesting to note that *Principals For Our Changing Schools* places the Instruction domain before the Curriculum Design domain. This is not a criticism. In fact, I agree this is the proper psychological order to follow. Too often the curriculum drives the teaching rather than the reverse. On the other hand, the logical order would go in reverse. When we study schooling logically we must be concerned first with the *what*, then the *why*, and, finally, the *how* of the enterprise. *What* is to be learned? *Why* is it to be learned? *How* is it to be learned?

Following the thinking of Mortimer Adler, *What* is to be learned falls under three categories: (1) the kinds of knowledge to be acquired; (2) the kinds of skills to be developed; and (3) the kinds of understanding and insights to be achieved. Subject matter or course content is only a means to this triple end.

Turning to *Why* knowledge, skills, and understanding are to be learned, we come to the larger purpose of schooling. The three basic objectives of formal schooling are to help the young develop the knowledge, skills, and understanding required if they are going to be able to earn a living, be good citizens, and live a full life which includes a lifelong love of learning.

Moving on to the *How,* we can look at this from the perspective of the principals, as we have been doing in this book. The prime task of the principal in his or her role as the "principal teacher" is to improve the quality of instruction. In Chapter 8, we were able to share some insights on how the principal should gain and use the knowledge, skills, and understanding necessary to carry out the delegation of this most important mission. In Chapter 9, we discussed the role of the principal in the *How* of teaching, and now, in the final chapter, we take up curriculum—the *What* of teaching.

When discussing teaching we mentioned that many people are afraid to use the phrase "to teach." We learned from Moran that this fear arises because all teaching is a moral activity. It involves a power relationship and that makes it subject to moral scrutiny. If teachers are called upon to make a series of moral judgments on *How* to teach, so, too, are the groups or individuals who decide *What* shall be taught. Curriculum Designers bear a tremendous moral responsibility because their decisions on *What* to teach greatly influence the teachers in their decisions on *How* to teach.

As principals you know how unfair it is to ask a fifth grade teacher to "cover the matter" contained in an overly-filled, rigidly-planned curriculum which fails to take into consideration the students' readiness to assimilate this mass of knowledge and information. Teachers held accountable for teaching an excessively full curriculum, and realizing that end of course tests will sample all the material, feel compelled to use the didactic approach 80% of the class time to "cover the matter." When seminar or coaching approaches are given short-shrift because of the compulsion to teach for tests, the students who need these aids are deprived and frequently fall behind. The students who need coaching and seminars most are usually found in the top third and the bottom third of the class. The top third need a diet of richer material which admits of deeper understanding in order to remain challenged. The bottom third starves from lack of study skills and enriched life experiences, hindering them in the race to cover the material.

To a large extent the learner's future is in the hands of the curriculum designers. A well-planned and implemented curriculum will contribute positively to the students continued learning in adult life. A poorly planned curriculum will make teaching more difficult and have the disastrous effect of killing any desire for future learning. Principals are beginning to be consulted about curriculum so they need all the help they can get in curriculum design. Only when principals and teachers are active partners with the central office and the State Education Department in designing curriculum will we be in a position to put the *What*, *Why*, and *How* together while giving the students' needs our highest priority.

No longer can principals allow overstuffed curricula, glossy text books, rigid daily schedules, standardized tests, and other adjuncts, intended as means to learning, become the end goal. As means these should be subservient to the true end of schooling which is to help students learn to love learning. If the school is effective, students will have for the rest of their lives the ability and desire to continue educating themselves to earn a decent living, to function as good citizens, and to live a full and worthwhile life. Curricula which for any reason kill the teachers' and students' love for learning are a menace. Bad curricula sabotage the very goal they claim to be working to achieve. It is imperative that principals and teachers have more input into the design of curricula. No true site management is possible without some control of curriculum.

Perrone goes as far as saying that if teaching is to be a rewarding and challenging profession, principals and teachers must make the key decisions about curriculum as it unfolds in the school and classroom. If learning is to be connected and relevant to students' intentions and needs, the curriculum will require a high level of flexibility. Only when we see teachers and their principals as curriculum-makers in the fullest sense deciding *What* and *How* to teach, will we see schools become effective in teaching students to love learning for a lifetime.

The definition of Curriculum Design in Domain #9 of *Principals For Our Changing Schools*, should prove most helpful to principals as they strive to work with their teachers to design curricula tailored to the needs of individual students:

> "Curriculum Design: Understanding major curriculum design models; interpreting school district curricula; initiating needs analyses; planning and implementing with staff a framework for instruction; aligning curriculum with anticipated outcomes; monitoring social and technological developments as they affect curriculum; adjusting content as needs and conditions change." (18)

Until quite recently "the curriculum" was the prerogative of the State Board and State Department of Education joined by the individual district superintendents. When I went to high school in 1934, there were three very distinct curricula in the same school building with a fourth in a building on the other side of the city. In our main building with 3,000 students, we had a college preparatory curriculum, a commercial (secretarial) curriculum for girls not going to college, and a general curriculum for noncollege bound boys which consisted of various shop courses and a few academic classes taught in a less demanding manner. Few boys remained in the general curriculum after they were 16 because it was easy to get highly paid factory jobs. In our "smoke stack" city only about 25% of the students who started with me in first grade graduated from high school, and only about 25% of that group went on for higher education. Less than one in 10 who started school with me went on to college. The high school had a clear mandate in the 1930s. Give your best to the select few who are college bound. Give good business and office training to the girls who will work as clerks and secretaries, and keep the shop boys off the streets. Across town there was a Trade School in which boys learned some of the basic trades: masonry, carpentry, welding, metal shop, plumbing, electrical work, etc.

The four different curricula were carved in stone and came down from the State Department and the District School superintendent. A student could go down the ladder from college preparatory to general, but I never heard of anyone ever going from trade school or general course to college preparatory. In a sense, we did informally what Europe did formally—we had a cutoff period for students at about 13 years of age. A few meant for a life of leisure and learning entered the college preparatory curriculum and the large majority were trained to work and vote.

The teaching I received in high school was neither rewarding nor challenging. The teachers seemed to go through the dull curriculum routine without any visible signs of excitement or delight. They weren't learning anything new themselves or gave no indication of it. They had no discretion over what they taught. It was the same stuff every semester. The students just did the minimum. Everyone who stayed in school miraculously graduated. I suffered through 4 years of the most uninspiring Latin classes you could imagine. There were dull English and French classes too. I nominate Ancient History as the most boring of the lot.

Even then the English teacher used commercially crafted multiple choice tests to check on our reading assignment—*A Tale of Two Cities* and *Silas Marner,* among others. Some bright kids discovered that the last letter of the last word in the question, was the same as the letter identifying the correct answer among the five offered in the multiple-choice question. This made correcting our tests easier for the teacher and freed her from reading the assigned works herself. Of course, it also freed the students from learning anything. Here was a class of college prep students passing English Literature tests without even reading the assignments. The classes were large, so we had almost no papers to write. We did not complain. Neither teachers nor students were active learners. It was not a Learning Organization.

On paper the written curriculum I followed in high school looked like the classical curriculum used in prestigious prep schools. But there was a giant difference between implemented curricula in those schools and in mine. I hope the difference will become clearer as we review the history of curriculum design in the U.S.

A CURRICULUM IS REALLY A RACE TRACK

In one of those sleepy Latin classes I did learn that "curere" was a verb meaning "to run." Later I learned the word curriculum was derived from the same verb and referred primarily to a race track or race course on which runners competed to see who could run the fastest. According to *Principals For Our Changing Schools*, the first time "curriculum" was used in the sense of a course of studies found within a school was in the University of Leiden in 1582. The authorities in that old university wanted to strengthen institutional order and discipline by controlling the structure of courses of study. This kind of institutional control over teachers has a long history.

In the year 1213, Pope Innocent III ruled that university professors—not church officials—were the experts who could control curriculum and license teachers. From the 13th century, curriculum has reigned supreme as the means by which those in power, like legislators, educational administrators, boards of education, state departments of education, and accrediting agencies, exert their power to control the running of the school. Since the current U.S. revolution in education begun in 1984, the battle has raged over who will control curriculum. Any child can control a huge bull if he can get hold of the ring in its nose. With schools it is much the same. The design of curriculum is the ring in the school's nose. Control it and you control the school.

Here we are, 780 years after Pope Innocent's ruling, still caught in the same push and pull over who will decide *What* and *How* to teach. If teaching is a moral activity and teaching is greatly influenced by curriculum, then curriculum design is also a moral matter. Principals must get into the battle and have a voice in how the curriculum is crafted and how much leeway it should allow to teachers and students.

In 1918, F. Bobbitt published a book in Boston entitled *The Curriculum*. It had great influence in its day. Bobbitt called for a study of society and the unmet needs of its people. The results of this study would be the basis for the school curriculum. For 30 years a mass influx of Irish, Italian, German, Scandinavian, Polish, Russian, and other immigrants had been flooding into the schools on the east coast, as well as in Chicago, Cleveland, St. Louis, Minneapolis, Toledo, and Pittsburgh. As today California is overwhelmed with waves of immigrants entering their schools, so the eastern and midwestern schools in the first third of this century had to cope with the flood of immigrant sons and daughters. They decided to teach them English so they could communicate and Civics so they could vote. The schools all taught practical skills so they could get a job. Mostly, the schools aimed to Americanize them. With the small elite who were aspiring to become doctors, lawyers, clergymen, scientists, and teachers, the schools used a classical liberal arts curriculum. For the rest, it was a kind of Life Adjustment Curriculum.

Unfortunately, by this time liberal education as it was known over the centuries had started to unravel and fall apart. At the turn of the century it started to slip, and by 1920s it was almost unrecognizable. When I was introduced to this marvelous source of learning in the 1930s, the purveyors of liberal education had turned it into a dry counting of verbs and adjectives. The spirit of inquiry was squeezed out of classical studies. The classicists envying the prestige of the physical scientists decided to ape their methods. They started to apply the scientific approach to the study of the classics. They dissected Dante the way the biologists dissected a frog. Something essential was lost in the process. In my high school, I learned to translate Caesar, Cicero, and Ovid from Latin, but I never learned to appreciate what they were communicating. It became anything but liberal or freeing.

Mortimer Adler is the voice of one crying in the wilderness, calling America back to a classical education with his Paideia Proposal. He and his colleague, Robert Hutchins, raised their voices in the 1940s and 1950s, begging educators to help students become proficient in the liberal arts so they could share in the Great Conversation with the best thinkers who shaped Western Civilization. They may prevail one day and all Americans will get 11 or 12 years of liberal education before they specialize. Though they must specialize in a complex technical world, they also must read, write, speak, listen, think, and understand the language that unites us, not just the jargon that separates us.

Between World War I and World War II, school curriculum limped along in the U.S. with little change. The same curriculum that structured the schools I attended in the '20s and '30s remained unchanged until a dozen years after World War II. In 1957, the Russians launched Sputnik and we

Americans were humiliated. We were losing the cold war. We had marvelously constructed rockets far superior to the Soviets but we didn't have the solid fuel capacity to catapult them into orbit. The Russian scientists bested our scientists. They must have better schools. We must revolutionize our schools. At the time, I was teaching in the university and I can remember the uproar. The school curriculum had to be totally overhauled, and science and math were going to play a key role in the education of all students. Millions of dollars, via the National Defense Education Act, were poured into the schools to implement the "New Math" and to upgrade science, foreign language, and technical subjects.

Educational uproar ushered in a new wave of mistrust of classroom teachers. At the 1962 National Academy of Science conference, Jerome Bruner urged that all students be taught the structure of the disciplines. National curriculum committees created an avalanche of new materials in math and science. These new materials were forged by academics and scientists in such a way as to make them "teacher proof." These well meaning intellectuals, who functioned far from the smell of the chalk, had very unrealistic ideas about the suitability of their materials for existing schools. It was another case of a quick fix for a longstanding problem. Starting in 1962, there has been a growing belief, voiced by many, that public school teachers are intellectually limited and, therefore, discretion must be taken away from them. The power should be given to a higher centralized agency. Central Office staffs multiplied at an alarming rate and played a heavy supervisory role. If teachers were that bad, many reasoned, school systems would have to rely on curriculum designers, text book writers, and test constructors to protect the students from them. Since the early 1960s, programs have been "top down," not originating in the school buildings. It is only now, in the 1990's, that educators are acknowledging that principals and teachers must be trained and empowered to take back control of the curriculum if school renewal is to succeed.

There were two movements which rocked the curriculum boat since 1962. Skinner and the Child Development camp both had their days in the sun. Skinner, the prototype behaviorist, introduced programmed learning and this caused some temporary ripples in the design of curricula. But by the 1980s, the emphasis had shifted away from strict behaviorist experimentalism to the developmental and cognitive learning models. More recently, Brookover and Edmonds have called attention to the fact that school curricula and instructional programs are embedded in the community and culture, and that individuals and social groups acquire and use information differently. We then began to hear of "cognitive thinking skills" and "learning styles." We were reminded that not all students develop at the same rate or learn in the same ways. We were acknowledging that all students can learn effectively given the proper learning conditions and time frame. Student centered curricula were initiated and touted in the "mastery learning" and "effective schools" literature. What goes around comes around.

Which brings us back to the purpose of this chapter. I want to help principals and teachers, who themselves are embedded in the community and culture, who know the parents and students, who smell the chalk each day, to cope with the added challenge of designing curriculum which will be integral to the school's larger purpose. This loosening of central control over curriculum makes it possible for stakeholders in the local school to create a Learning Organization.

WHAT THE PRINCIPAL DOES TO IMPROVE THE SCHOOL CURRICULUM

So far we have solely discussed why the principal must take an active part in designing the curriculum. We have not yet offered any guidance on how he or she will go about doing this. *Principals For Our Changing Schools* assumes that in progressive school systems, local school staffs, under the direction of the principal, will engage in reflective and critical analysis to redesign curricula for their unique group of students. I would go further and say that in all school systems, principals are beginning to be called upon to take a more active part in curriculum design. No longer does the principal merely oversee the implementation of curricula that have been developed by commercial publishers, state education departments, and other external bodies.

If principals are to be prepared to carry out these added curriculum duties, they will have to have training and support. The first thing principals must understand is curriculum theory and practice from a historical perspective. Even our very brief review makes it clear that principals and teachers should be given the power to design and redesign the curriculum. With that metanoia or mind shift we see the beginning step in the long journey of school renewal. What took 100 years to wind down, will take at least 50 or 60 to wind up and set right. Our universal educational system like our democracy is still in its infancy.

Adler makes a strange prediction. He says that it will take us until 2040 to get the schools where they should be. In one sense this prediction is discouraging, yet I believe it is realistic. This country of ours is the oldest functioning democracy in the world but, as Adler reminds us, we are still not a full democracy by any stretch of the imagination. The U.S. made a huge step toward becoming a full-fledged democracy in the 1960s with the passage of the Civil Rights Legislation and the War On Poverty. We still have a long way to go in our society and our schools before we can honestly say that we are functioning as a true democracy. Our schools will be fully democratic only when we can deliver a quality liberal education and make it accessible to all children.

How can we get principals ready to join their teachers in designing and redesigning curricula in a school? *Principals For Our Changing Schools* offers principals a model to integrate the major initiatives they can and must use to improve school curriculum (17). Studying the figure on the next page, we see "The Written Curriculum" is at the apex, "The Taught Curriculum" on the lower left hand side, and "The Tested Curriculum" on the lower right hand side. In the middle we read "Quality Control of School Work" and note how the arrows go in both directions connecting the three points of the triangle. The model helps principals to conceptualize the problem. The principal and teachers must take curriculum to be a field of practice which should consist of the delivery of certain services, and the resolution of certain kinds of problems that arise in schools.

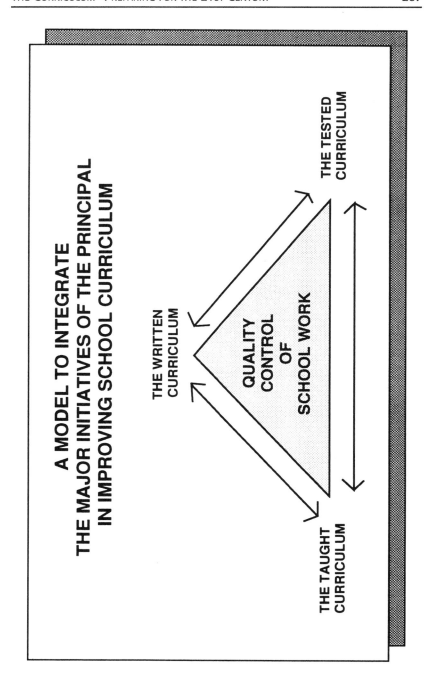

Curriculum work primarily concerns itself with those services and problems which are related to the purposes and content of the school's programs. There is no way of separating the content you choose to teach from the reason why you are teaching it. Too often in the past, the curriculum designers, starting with their own preconceived notions, used their power to impose certain favored content without taking into consideration the specific goals or the particular mix of stake-holders in each school. The curriculum designers should work in the practical realm, figuring out the best content and service, and determining how these should be organized in time, in relation to one another, and in relation to the stakeholders. How ludicrous it was to impose a curriculum content without taking these things into consideration, yet we did it for years. When it didn't prove effective, it was easy to find scapegoats—teachers, students, parents, etc. It was illogical to say, "We had a terrific curriculum but the teachers didn't teach it well and the students couldn't learn it." The only proof of the existence of teaching is the presence of learning. The only way we can judge that a curriculum is worthwhile is that the students who are subjected to it are learning how to learn and showing interest in furthering their own education.

Curriculum problems are practical problems, the kinds with which the principal and teachers should be engaged. Stakeholders will never be finished fine-tuning curricula. In a Learning Organization all stakeholders firmly believe that curricula need to change regularly in order to keep the stake-holders ahead of the societal change curve. Our only hope is that by 2040 we will have the feedback loop in place so the stakeholders will take it for granted that everyone on the Learning Teams will be involved daily in making sure that the curriculum is doing its job. Where the curriculum is failing, it will be changed and some more suitable content or service will replace it. Curricula won't be carved in stone for the sake of text books.

What I like most about the model we are discussing is that it can be entered from any direction, and is contextually grounded. This is a process that is relational and systems-oriented. All the stakeholders are actively involved and they work in teams interdependently. The goal of the curriculum design team is clearly printed in the center of the model: Quality Control of School Work. It acknowledges that the curriculum cannot be written in stone because it must dance with the purposes of the school and the changing demands of the environment. If the principal thinks of starting with the Written Curriculum and moving clockwise, he or she will see immediately that this Written Curriculum must be seen in relation with the Tested Curriculum. Continuing in the same direction, the principal comes to the Taught Curriculum and sees immediately that there has to be a relation between the Tested Curriculum and the Taught Curriculum. Since the Written Curriculum and the Tested Curriculum can be observed objectively, it will be easy to blame the Taught Curriculum if the Tested Curriculum doesn't measure up to the Written Curriculum. Hasn't this been the way in the past? We have a wonderful curriculum and the tests show that the students are failing so it must be the fault of the teachers. Or perhaps it is the students or their parents who are at fault.

Of the many things I learned from my 4 day workshop with Edwards Deming, one of the most helpful was his insistence that it is a waste of time to point the finger and assign blame to one or the other of the stakeholders. When we start to think in a systems- oriented manner, we can admit that if the students don't do well on the Tested Curriculum, the cause is probably systemic, rather than individual. It could be that one or more of the three curricula—Written, Tested, and Taught—are out of sync with the others, with the teachers, students, parents, and larger society. When the designing of curriculum is done far away from the site in which it is to be practiced, this type of systems imbalance is the rule rather than the exception.

How can we miss the lesson taught us by the U.S.S.R.? The Soviets were intelligent people, world-class thinkers. How could they allow their farming and manufacturing capacity to wither away to the point that they had to import food and other products? In analogy with curriculum design, it was their Communist Ideology of centralized planning and their refusal to reward effort which blinded them to the realities of life. The Communist theory fell apart in practice despite their 5-year plans. The same thing has happened to our educational system.

The belief that curriculum could be designed by people far from the smell of the chalk, then carved in stone and imposed on schools made up of stakeholders from grossly different socio-economic and demographic backgrounds, was unrealistic to say the least. It failed long ago. We are only now like the Soviets, admitting our mistakes.

GOOD CURRICULUM DESIGN DEMANDS THAT THE PRINCIPAL USE SYSTEMS THINKING

You will recall that in previous chapters I frequently used Senge's terms: Shared Vision, Personal Mastery, Mental Models, and Team Learning. I promised that in the last chapter we would take up the last, and perhaps the most important, of the five disciplines—Systems Thinking. Senge calls it his fifth discipline. He claims that the only way to build a Learning Organization is by utilizing an ensemble of the five disciplines. To apply his approach to the principals' task, we could say the only way a principal can change his school into a Learning Organization is by using all five disciplines in concert.

When the U.S. Hockey team pulled a giant upset in the Olympic Games some years ago by beating a much more experienced Soviet team, it electrified the American people, but what it did for the American players and coaches is even more astonishing. Team members were bonded for life. They felt that they had been a part of something much larger than themselves. They felt close to each other because they experienced something nobody else had. It must be the same with the *Endeavor* crew astronauts who did such an impressive job repairing the Hubble telescope. With both teams, wherever they live, wherever they travel, people will know them as members of the U.S. Hockey team which beat the U.S.S.R. or the *Endeavor* crew that worked in space for hours to fix the telescope. It was the most strikingly meaningful experience in their lives. The hockey team now believes in miracles. The players could never doubt that David can beat Goliath. The astronauts believed in them-selves and in the whole Houston space team which got them there and back. Both teams realized how their pursuit of the five disciplines helped accomplish their goals. It is the same with Curriculum Design. We see how all five disciplines—

Shared Vision, Personal Mastery, Mental Models, Team Learning, and Systems Thinking—serve to create a Learning
Organization.

I am willing to bet that many of you principals have had a
similar experience. The content of the experience (olympic
hockey games, space shuttle experience, starting a new school,
coaching a winning team, launching a successful writing
program) is less important than the process by which different
people buy into a Shared Vision, use their highly developed
Personal Mastery in the service of the vision, willingly subject
their Mental Models to open scrutiny, put inquiry above
advocacy, strive together as Team Learners, and use Systems
Thinking to constantly focus on accomplishing the whole team
vision rather than on some selfishly interesting personal part.
When Team Learners utilize Systems Thinking, they don't allow
any particular subsystem to take precedence over the whole
mission. Each team member sacrifices willingly some of the
things he likes and does well in order to be a team player. This
is the secret of getting great things accomplished. It is the secret
of designing a balanced curriculum. It is what should be taught
from preschool through grad school, and I never heard a word
of it during my almost 70 years of schooling. I can think of no
better way to help principals lead their stakeholders in the
design of curricula than by explaining what Systems Thinking
is all about. If principals can learn to put the five disciplines
together and teach other stakeholders this secret, our curriculum design would be effective and schools would become
Learning Organizations.

Systems Thinking makes understandable the most subtle
aspect of a Learning Organization, *i.e.*, the new way team
members begin to perceive themselves and their world. At the
core of a Learning Organization is a shift of mind (metanoia).
It can be described this way: We seem for the first time to
perceive ourselves no longer as disconnected from the world
like a single pebble or grain of sand lying passively on a huge
beach, but rather as a highly integrated, actively participating
agent (dreamer-doer) accomplishing something (making a
vision real). We feel alive and fulfilled because we perceive ourselves as related to and contributing with others to something
much too big to be realized by an individual. Best of all, the

Shared Vision we are making possible is the right thing to do. It will help many others as well as ourselves. It will outlive us. In a sense it will immortalize us.

In a true Learning Organization, Team Learners are continually discovering how they create their reality. As long as they hold onto the belief that their Mental Models of reality are the reality itself instead of a representation of it, they can't have a metanoia or mind shift. How can they learn when they know it all? Learners can't learn anything until they begin to have some doubts. Then they are willing, at least temporarily, to suspend their Mental Models. They have to allow others to see, react to, criticize, and amend their cherished Mental Models. This happens only when they are willing to enter a conversation or dialogue, and actually begin to express their opinions and listen to the opinions of other Team Learners. They begin to acknowledge that they may not have a corner on the whole truth. It is only then that they become able to learn, to experience metanoias.

The purpose of a school is to allow teachers and students to work together to make possible mind shifts. If that is true of the school in general, what does it say about the purpose of curriculum design? A curriculum under-stood the way *Principals For Our Changing Schools* explains it, has but one purpose—to aid the process of learning in all stake-holders or Team Learners. Effectively designed curricula accomplish this goal, others do not.

If I am correct, the most important first step for curriculum designers is to hold the vision of creating a learning atmosphere in which all stakeholders will be encouraged to continue learning throughout their lives. It is obvious that the principal as "principal teacher" must take the lead and include all Team Learners in curriculum design. Does this mean some representatives of the students should be included? Of course it does. It also means that all the teachers and representatives of the school staff, parents, and other loyal supporters should be included.

Real learning gets to the heart of what it means to be a human person. The purpose of learning is to recreate ourselves. The youngsters who come to school with "unschooled minds" need to test many of the things they already "know," experience some metanoias, and begin to understand more deeply their universe and the place they hold in it. A good curriculum does more than strengthen the institution's order and discipline, it offers the teachers and students an opportunity to deepen and broaden their understanding, and open up rich veins for further learning. Such a curriculum will lead both teachers and students through countless mind shifts or metanoias in which they will change their "world views" many times on the way to becoming wiser, and we hope, better human persons.

HUTCHINS HELPS WITH CURRICULUM DESIGN

Hutchins insisted that a liberally educated person should have a mind that could operate well in all fields. He felt that although specialization had many advantages as far as advancing technological frontiers, it should not be purchased at the cost of a general or liberal education. If the best minds don't have enough breadth of language and learning to be able to speak to anyone not in their specialty, our world will become more and more like the Tower of Babel. It has happened. Witness the spectacle of inarticulate experts obfuscating issues. The task of the future is building a community which demands that all stakeholders are able to see the big picture or vision, and have the communication skills necessary to be Team Learners. To do this we will need a curriculum which is inclusive rather than exclusive.

I personally have always found Hutchins most helpful when he explains that the liberally educated person should feel at home both in the world of ideas and in the world of practical affairs. It seems the liberally educated person understands the relationship between the two, and has a broad enough language base to speak and listen to all the community builders, regardless of their specialties.

It is impossible to design a Systems Thinking curriculum without considering the liberal arts themselves. When one explains that the liberal artist must learn to read, write, speak, listen, understand, and think, most teachers agree that is exactly what they had in mind. They refer to these activities as the "basics," but they are truly the liberal arts. Actually, the method of liberal education is the liberal arts, and the outcome of liberal education is discipline in those arts. A credible curriculum must prepare students to reckon, measure and manipulate matter, quantity, and motion in order to predict, produce, and exchange. We still live in a tradition in which all of us are called to be liberal artists. The schools still half-heartedly practice the liberal arts. However, many teachers have had little exposure to them and, as a result, they are easily seduced into filling the curriculum with all kinds of specialized subjects more suited to college while curtailing reading, writing, speaking, listening, thinking, and understanding.

Our western tradition demands that we understand our "roots" as well as we can in order to understand ourselves. Hutchins makes it clear that we can't decide whether we are going to be human beings (the die has been cast by our DNA). The only choice we have is whether we will be ignorant, undeveloped humans or beings who seek to reach the highest point we can as humans. Hutchins finally brings it down to this question. Our choice is whether we will be poor liberal artists or good ones. What choice do we have? We are obligated by our western tradition to see that everyone has the opportunity to gain their fullest measure of the liberal arts. Since the acquisition of the liberal arts is an intrinsic part of human dignity, then the democratic ideal of the west demands that we design school curricula that open up the liberal arts to every child and adult. Only then can they enter the Great Conversation with the thinkers who shaped and formed our western tradition characterized as it is by the spirit of inquiry.

SYSTEMS THINKING YIELDS A CURRICULUM WHICH HIGHLIGHTS WHOLES INSTEAD OF PARTS

Should curriculum be concerned only about excellence in the past? Impossible if we use a Systems Thinking approach. This way of thinking makes it clear that the Grand System that holds it all together goes from 15 billions years ago up to the present nanosecond, and on into the vague future. The whole ideal of a school is to help students make connections between the past, the present, and the future. Most students are very much a part of their present culture. What they need from school are the skills and knowledge necessary for critically appraising their current culture milieu in the light of the past. They don't need to be taught in school what their world is screaming at them. They do need guidance in separating the wheat from the chaff. They need all the help they can get in the liberal arts and from the classics so they can make sane judgments, form healthy communities, and craft their futures. They are bombarded with facts, information, experiences, advertising, sermonettes, peer pronouncements, messages from films, radio, tapes, CDs, TV. What a good curriculum should do is help the students sort, sift, and grade the messages in the light of a value system that has a shelf-life longer than 12 weeks. They need a curriculum that helps them make better life choices and judgments.

A Systems Thinking curriculum will stress wholeness. The curriculum designers will find modern thinkers who have integrated analysis and feeling, as well as intellect and physical competence. How much better would each of us be if we had learned one of the practical arts like farming, painting, shoe making, electrical work, masonry, carpentry? Early in the history of modern Israel it was the custom for all young people to learn a trade even if they planned a professional career. It was a good way of keeping in touch with nature, learning patience, and respecting the limits placed on the artist by the materials employed. Best of all, it gave the young Israelis the confidence that they could do something practical not just think abstractly. It broke down the white collar–blue collar cast system. Touching nature and respecting her limits set up a healthy friction between an alert mind and practical experience. Curricula that stress only "abstract learning" or "book learning" separates the students from the facts of life. Often it promotes pedantry and mediocrity. How often have principals scratched their heads when they watched 18-year-olds graduate realizing that many had failed to master any particular skill or manual competence?

The Systems Thinking curriculum will overcome one of the defects of the modern "cafeteria style" curriculum—its disconnectedness. The subjects in many school curricula look like unhooked freight cars lying around a huge railroad yard in complete disarray, having no reason for where they are. Reality can't be divided into distinct subjects. Reality can't be known and understood without grasping relations between entities. That's the reason I have stressed the advantages of overarching themes like Global or International Education. The Performing Arts School is another example of a Systems Thinking curriculum which links all the offerings into a meaningful whole. We usually don't think that way. Frank Hughes' Learning Teams know they can't create a Learning Organization if the members are each pursuing specifics that bear no relation to the whole. That is why they keep referring curricula decisions to the Global Education theme. It is as if Global Education is the satellite, and the individual subjects and topics are beamed to the satellite to see how they fit together and support each other.

Frank Hughes' Learning Teams now see how much in the past the subjects and specialties in their school were pursued with both teachers and students wearing blinders. Looking at the Global Model has helped them realize that organized knowledge is better understood when it is connected with a larger context. Communication thrives in this broader unifying atmosphere. How does the English reading class fit in with Global Education? What about singing in chorus? Beam it to the satellite and see how it fits in. Ask why in Japan and Hungary all children sing together in choruses? How do the Japanese and the Hungarians view Art and Music in their schools, and connect them to the study of reading in their language courses? The Japanese and Hungarians must make more connections than we do. Could we start thinking of Art, Music, and Dance as staples to be used in every class regardless of the subject area? This would cut down on the kind of specialization which undermines communication. It would also be a start in implementing what we already know about the Seven Intellectual Competencies all students and teachers share. Here is an opportunity to integrate language, mathematical, musical, and spatial abilities with the kinesthetic. Some people just communicate better in music, dance, drawing, and gymnastics than they do in word or number.

In making our curriculum more relevant we must provide a sober view of the world without inducing despair. Believe me, this is not easy. Students should be exposed to the annual edition of Lester Brown's *World Watch,* which is the ecologists' report card on the global sustainability. In it, global environmental and ecological conditions are honestly appraised. Reading it is like being hit with a pail of cold water. I don't have the time to develop the ideas here, but I do recommend that the new curricula have plenty of content about the problem of Global sustainability. We educators must join with the students and become architects of sustainable communities. Students can make a real difference in controlling the polluting of the planet. Most of them do care deeply about it. Although the whole subject of ecological disaster is depressing, it is an area in which we still can do something about the future. My sister-in-law, who teaches Environmental Ethics at the college level, says students are beginning to see how much they can do to stem ecological disaster. They quickly grasp the idea that to be sustainable, a society must be able to live on its income not on its capital. Elementary students who are exposed to the ecological approach to global problems take quickly to the idea of recycling. How can we in good conscience design curricula which fail to inform students of ecological problems so relevant to them?

We would be remiss if we didn't include in the curriculum some samples of the classical treasures of the past with its excellent pieces on literature, philosophy, theology, science, history, mathematics, drama. This gives the students the opportunity to join the great conversation with the best thinkers who formed our western tradition. However, we would be equally remiss if we didn't introduce them to the works of our best thinkers today. Here we can bring in works of a more widely multicultural kind. It was a Russian, Vladimir Vernadsky, who published *The Biosphere,* in 1926, which earned him the title of the father of Ecological Interdependence. No child should go through school without being exposed to the thinking of this genius. Vernadsky foresaw, almost 70 years ago, the implications of a planetary system of life. He opened the door to the postmodern age and closed in on the modern age which since 1648 favored a nation-state system.

No student entering the 21st century should be ignorant of what Rachel Carson foretold in *The Silent Spring* (1962), the indiscriminate use of weed killers and insecticides constituted a hazard to wildlife and to human beings.

Why should we use wars as markers to highlight the stages of history? Why start with Homer? Why not use the longer time frame and highlight the positive in human develop-ment? Systems Thinking curricula should cover the past, present, and future.

When we take a Systems Thinking approach to curriculum design, or to anything for that matter, we are forced to take a sweeping view going back and forth, up and down, in and out, over and around. As we prepare our students to live in the Global Village, we need to give them a curriculum which will open their heads, hearts, and hands to all the reality in the cosmos. Frank Hughes and his Learning Teams are overawed when they take this sweeping view. They are discouraged because they know so little about what is really happening in their world. They know they can never teach the students all the literature, science, math, history, geography, civics, art, music, astronomy, they really should. When they moan the longest, Frank gets up and makes his favorite speech:

"The reason we feel so badly is because we see so clearly. There is a much worse state. Many educators don't yet see how fast change is coming, and how much their students depend on them for help in learning to live with it. If we keep our heads, work together as Team Learners toward our Shared Vision, try to develop Personal Mastery, allowing our Mental Models to be surfaced, tested, and changed as needed, we can learn more ourselves, and we can be models to the students, helping them, through our Systems Thinking curricula, to see themselves and their world in a more realistic way. This is what Global Education is all about. We can give them hope that they can make a difference in their futures. If they are willing to work with us, we now feel we can give them samples of excellence from the classics to appreciate and work on. We can show them how to read, write, speak, listen, think, and understand the past, present, and future. We can help them develop all seven of their intellectual competencies and be ready to educate themselves through the rest of their lives on this planet. That is why we are trying to form a Learning Organization. It is the only type of organization that will survive in the next century."

Frank has given this speech over 200 times in church basements, school halls, gyms, and living rooms. He and his staff are prophets in the truest sense of the word. They are trying to sound a warning to parents, teachers, students, and others that nothing less than a Systems Thinking approach to education will work. We will change our schools into Learning Organizations in which all stakeholders continue to learn, or we will fail our students miserably. Frank and his troops will make many mistakes, but I am certain they will be successful in the long run. They inspire me.

Today Systems Thinking is needed more than ever because we are all becoming overwhelmed by complexity. We now have the capacity to create more information than anyone can absorb, to foster greater independence than anyone can manage, and to ratchet up the rate of change faster than anyone can run. Perhaps we should keep in mind as we design curricula that this complexity has a tendency to undermine students' self-confidence and sense of responsibility. They may have the inclination to throw up their hands in frustration, and say they can't be expected to do anything about the problems in the world since they are too complex. Their frustration is perfectly understandable but it is dangerous since it leads to a feeling of helplessness and apathy.

Systems Thinking is the best antidote we have for this condition. Systems Thinking offers people the opportunity to look beneath the superficial complexities and to understand the "structures" that underlie them. A tree is very complex until you see that it is made up of a trunk, branches, and roots deep in the ground. Understanding the underlying structures can help our students discover the higher and lower leverage points. This gives them the opportunity to make changes instead of remaining passive. Nothing gives people more self-confidence than the realization that they have the power to change things which influence their daily lives. Systems Thinking is the first step in this direction.

As I bring this chapter to an end, I want to acknowledge my heavy debt to Scott Thomson and his associates. They have defined the 21 domains in *Principals For Our Changing Schools* and given us a Systems Thinking approach to preparing new principals and updating practicing principals. I hope every school administrator makes use of their excellent study. My debt to Peter Senge is almost as great. I have leaned heavily on his research in *The Fifth Discipline* to offer you the unifying concept of a Learning Organization and the five disciplines which, if pursued, can create such an organization. School administrators could profit greatly from reading this work.

It was with live principals constantly before my mind that I put together this series of 10 essays. I have tried to help principals use all the skills and knowledge they have to turn their schools into Learning Organizations. I chose the first nine domains of skills and knowledge suggested in *Principals For Our Changing Schools* and tried to apply them to actual school settings. Having taught over 1,500 public school principals and 350 assistant principals during the last 10 years I had plenty of material. I guess it is apparent that I have grown to love and respect these heroes. I am constantly amazed at the number of principals who are rising to the challenge and accomplishing wondrous transformations in their schools.

SUMMATION

Throughout this book, I have focused on the principal as the Principal Teacher whose chief task is to improve the quality of instruction. I offer the principals a way of accomplishing this through the five disciplines: Shared Vision, Personal Mastery, Mental Models, Team Learning, and, finally, Systems Thinking. It appears clear to me that any principal who works diligently at assimilating the 21 domains from Scott Thomson's book and seriously commits to the five disciplines suggested by Senge, will be well-equipped to become a transformative leader capable of changing his or her school into a Learning Organization. *We want the principals to be transformative leaders, who are able to recognize real needs, spot contradictions among values and between values and practice, realign values, reorganize schools, and manage changes involved in the process, awaken stakeholders to the point where they are conscious of what they feel, and move learning team members to purposeful action.*

Marian Wright Edelman, president of the Childrens' Defense Fund tells us that children are drowning in the meaninglessness of a culture that rewards greed and guile and tells them life is about getting rather than giving. You and I know that our children deserve better than that. We can do better than that. I think of principals as point guards who, with the help of the other Team Learners, can turn the game around, converting tired, sluggish schools into vibrant Learning Organizations which offer teachers, students and parents safe communities in which they can really share love of learning for a lifetime.

QUESTIONS FOR REFLECTION

1. If teaching is to be a rewarding and challenging profession, principals and teachers must make the key decisions about curriculum as it unfolds in the school and classroom. How can you justify this statement? If you can't justify it, why not? Does the statement preclude national standards?

2. How did the mass influx of immigrants during a 30-year period in our history influence the design of curriculum? Are there similarities today?

3. Compare and contrast: the Written Curriculum, the Taught Curriculum, and the Tested Curriculum. Seen from a Systems Thinking approach, how could overstressing one of these lead to a disastrous imbalance? What if the Hidden Curriculum has more power than all others?

4. The first step for curriculum designers is to hold the vision of creating a learning atmosphere in which all stakeholders will be encouraged to continue learning throughout their lives. How does this approach differ from "covering the matter," "political correctness," or "cultural literacy?"

5. Do you think Hutchins' emphasis on teaching the liberal arts is elitist? How can he say our only choice is whether we will be good or poor liberal artists? How does he understand "artist?"

6. The whole ideal of a school is to help students make connections between the past, the present, and the future. They need the skills and knowledge necessary for critically appraising their current culture milieu in the light of the past and the future. How does the principal use that insight when designing curriculum?

7. The Systems Thinking approach to curriculum design will overcome one of the defects of the modern "cafeteria style" curriculum, its disconnectedness. How does an overarching theme help?

8. How can principals design curricula which will be as sensitive to the classical tradition of our past as it is to the formidable ecological future, and yet be relevant to the cultural multiplicity of the present? It isn't easy. How can they be sensitive to something that hasn't yet come into existence? Why start 15 billion years ago and try to project into the 22nd century? By definition a Learning Organization is creative and generative. It is always creating its own future. How?

REFERENCES

References are to *Principals For Our Changing Schools* (1993), edited by Scott D. Thomson, National Policy Board for Educational Administration, 4400 University Drive, Fairfax, VA 22030-4444 (703-993-3644).

(1)   Preface x
(2)   Preface xi
(3)   Domain 1, page 3
(4)   Domain 1, page 6
(5)   Domain 1, page 17
(6)   Domain 2, page 6
(7)   Domain 2, page 6
(8)   Domain 3, page 3
(9)   Domain 3, page 9
(10)   Domain 4, page 5
(11)   Domain 5, page 3
(12)   Domain 5, page 13
(13)   Domain 6, page 3
(14)   Domain 7, page 3
(15)   Domain 7, page 11
(16)   Domain 8, page 3
(17)   Domain 8, page 5
(18)   Domain 9, page 3
(19)   Domain 9, page 9

SUGGESTED READINGS

Adler, Mortimer J., *Reforming Education,* Macmillan, New York, 1988.

Berrry, Thomas, *The Dream of the Earth,* Sierra Club Books, San Francisco, 1990.

Deming, W. Edwards, *Out of the Crisis,* Massachusetts Institute of Technology, Center for Advanced Engineering, Cambridge, MA, 1982.

Dimnet, Ernest, *The Art of Thinking,* Premier Books, New York, 1962.

Edelman, Marian Wright, *The Measure of Our Success,* Beacon Press, Boston, 1992.

Fiske, Edward B., *Smart Schools, Smart Kids,* Simon & Schuster, New York, 1991.

Gardner, Howard, *Frames of Mind,* Basic Books, New York, 1983.

Gardner, Howard, *The Unschooled Mind,* Basic Books, New York, 1991.

Goodlad, John I., *A Place Called School,* McGraw-Hill, New York, 1986.

Grove, Andrew S., *High Output Management,* Random House, New York, 1983.

Hirsch, E.D., Jr., *Cultural Literacy,* Houghton Mifflin, Boston, 1987.

Moran, Gabriel, *Show How: An Inquiry into the Art of Teaching,* unpublished manuscript, New York, 1993.

Perrone, Vito, *A Letter to Teachers,* Jossey-Bass, San Francisco 1991.

Sizer, Theodore R., *Horace's School,* Houghton Mifflin, Boston, 1992.

Senge, Peter M., *The Fifth Discipline,* Doubleday, New York, 1990.

Tuchman, Barbara W., *The March of Folly,* Ballantine Books, New York, 1984.